Here is what church leaders are saying about *Her Calling*

This work is a masterpiece! Dr. Jamie Morgan speaks to some of the harder spaces women face as minis[illegible]d, Spirit-empowered, practical steps to [illegible]g. I recommend this book for women in all seasons of ministry.

—**CRYSTAL MARTIN**, National Director, Assemblies of God Network of Women Ministers

---

Half of God's army—women—stand on the sidelines, and God is beckoning them to take the field. They ask, "What do I need to do? How do I position myself? What do I need to know?" Jamie Morgan answers these questions and more. This is such a needed book to help women launch into action!

—**BARBARA J. YODER**, Founding and Lead Apostle, Shekinah Christian Church

---

Get ready to become all that God has called you to be for such a time as this. Dr Jamie Morgan is truly a Deborah and a mother to this generation. Read this book and put its words into practice, because your time is NOW!

—**DEHAVILLAND FORD**, Founder of 818 The Sign

You don't have to spend another minute wondering what your God-given calling looks like or how to fulfill it. Dr. Jamie Morgan mentors you to step out of the shadows and into the fullness of all God has called you to be. Filled with a wealth of personal experience and practical insight, *Her Calling* is truly transformative.

—**ANGELA DONADIO**, Ministry Leader, Author, and Host of the Make Life Matter Podcast

---

Dr. Jamie Morgan is truly a Trailblazer, and with *Her Calling* she has placed in our hands the opportunity to glean from her decades of experience and wisdom! As a woman called to ministry, this book challenged, inspired, and encouraged me to step further into my victorious destiny with courage and confidence to reap an end-time harvest of souls!

—**SUSANNE COX**, Co-founder, Legacy of Purpose

This is one the most profound books ever written on calling! It is a clear roadmap and complete guide to assure the discovery of your calling and destiny! It is practical, highly spiritual, and well written. I recommended this work for every believer—laity or clergy. It belongs in your library!

—**LANA HEIGHTLEY, DPM**, President and Founder, Women With A Mission

---

This is the most comprehensive book I have read regarding mentoring women. No matter where you are in your journey, *Her Calling* will activate, restore, transform, and challenge you. There's an old saying, "There's nothing like time in the saddle," referring to experiential wisdom. Jamie shares that kind of wisdom in this book.

—**REV., DR. MELONIE JANET MANGUM**, CEO, Partners for Transformation, Director, Aglow International Transformation

---

Dr. Jamie Morgan *reads the mail* of every woman minister who is hungry to be effective and fulfill her calling. She provides key components to equip us to serve the King of Kings as His daughter—called and anointed. You'll greatly benefit from Dr. Morgan's wisdom and experience. So grab a cup of coffee and *Her Calling*. You won't regret it!

—**REV. RENEÉ DUNCAN**, A NEUE NOW Ministries

Dr. Jamie Morgan skillfully equips the woman of God to pursue her calling through this brilliant book. She charges us to "Let's go! Let's go! Let's go!" This book will inspire and prepare women of all ages to fulfill their God-given callings.

—**MARGIE FLEURANT**, Margie Fleurant Ministries

There is a divine charge being released from God for His sons and daughters to rise up. And Dr. Jamie stands as an Apostolic voice to encourage, liberate, and equip women to become change agents for God. Regardless of season or ministry context, *Her Calling* is answered prayer for the many women struggling with a misplaced identity. And Jamie Morgan provides tools to move them—and all of us—forward.

—**REV., DR. ANTOINETTE ATTINSON**, Pastor, Author, International Speaker

I LOVED this book, and you will too! It is so timely and needed for women today. Jamie is that mentor every woman needs, and *Her Calling* provides to us important and practical guidance in every step and phase of our ministry journeys. Every woman believer should study this book to become a better disciple of Jesus Christ. Grab this book and don't let go!

—**MERRILY MADERO**, Colonel, Retired, U.S. Air Force, Ordained Minister, Assemblies of God; President, M3 International

---

Woman of God, get ready to be deeply challenged as Dr. Jamie Morgan catapults you into your calling and guides you on a journey to discover your purpose. *Her Calling* will assist you in fulfilling your God-ordained destiny. Through it you will learn to navigate pitfalls and be equipped and encouraged to accomplish your passion and greatly impact the world for the Glory of God.

—**CINDY PANEPINTO**, Upward Call Ministries

Dr. Jamie Morgan is being used powerfully by the Lord in this hour to call upon women of God to arise and go forth into their God-given destinies. I am excited to see this book written and highly recommend it to women everywhere! The time is now; the hour is late; and women of God must assume their roles in fulfilling The Great Commission!

—**KEITH COLLINS**, Generation Impact Ministries; Impact Global Fellowship

---

In *Her Calling,* Dr. Jamie has captured a clarion call to women that will define destinies for generations to come. Jamie Morgan provides valuable insight from her own personal experiences. And this book will not only awaken you but also resound the calling in your life and cause you to arise and walk it out with confidence as a daughter of the Most High God.

—**JANET DOUGLAS**, Apostolic Leader, Janet Douglas Ministries, Founder, Kingdom Glory Ministries / CityGate Indiana

In this book, Dr Jamie does a masterful job of addressing ladies about their callings—from the one who has yet to discover what that is, to the one who is developing in her calling, to the one who has engaged in her calling but has plateaued. Jamie shares wisdom to keep each lady moving forward in the purpose of God. Excellent read!.

—**BO SALISBURY**, Kingdom Culture International

With *Her Calling*, Dr. Jamie Morgan has written a most powerful and profound book. If you ever had questions about the call of God on your life and how to walk in that calling, you will certainly benefit from the wealth of wisdom this masterpiece provides. But just a word of warning—this book may cause you to realize some God-sized dreams for your life.

—**DONNA SPARKS**, Author, Evangelist, Revivalist, Founder of Story of Grace Prison Ministry

---

Jamie Morgan offers her faith-infused mentoring voice to rising women leaders through *Her Calling*. Compelled by her passion to launch other ministers, Jamie carefully outlines the obstacles women face in ministry, and she holds the reader's hand so she doesn't stumble on the pathway to becoming who God has called her to be. *Her Calling* demolishes the enemy's assault against women ministers and strengthens their resolve to allow nothing to stand in the way of their callings, purpose, or destinies.

—**REV. MELANIE BOUDREAU**, Advisor, Apostolic Intercessors Network

---

In *Her Calling,* Dr. Morgan shares wisdom from her ministry experience to guide the reader in her journey from her first, "Yes," along the road of growth, up the mountains, through the valleys of challenges (all the while staying the course and advancing the Kingdom of God), to the point of receiving the reader's rewards.

—**REV., DR. LAURIE VERVAECKE**, Pastor, The Well (Salt Lake City), President, Global Leadership Network

Her CALLING

A WOMAN'S GUIDE TO FULFILLING HER GOD-GIVEN DESTINY

FOREWORD BY J. LEE GRADY

DR. JAMIE MORGAN

BRIDGE LOGOS

Newberry, FL 32669

Bridge-Logos
Newberry, FL 32669

Her Calling:
A Woman's Guide to Fulfilling Her God-given Destiny
by Dr. Jamie Morgan

Printed in the United States of America.

Library of Congress Catalog Card Number: 2022947308

International Standard Book Number: 978-1-61036-080-7

Literary Agent and Editor,
L. Edward Hazelbaker
thewornkeyboard.com

Interior design: Kent Jensen, knail.com

Cover design: Ashley Morgan

VP 11/2022

DEDICATION

I dedicate this book to *You*, Lord Jesus. My prayer is that *Her Calling* will inspire, encourage, and challenge my granddaughters, Claire Abigail and Hannah Jane, as well as women everywhere, to walk in the fullness of their callings and take their places in the end-times harvest of souls.

FOREWORD

When I visited a group of unregistered church leaders in a city near Hong Kong almost 20 years ago, I discovered that between one-half to two-thirds of all church planters in China today are women. Along with their male colleagues, those women lead an estimated 25,000 people to Christ daily.

One evening during that trip I returned to my hotel room and discovered two of the female leaders waiting at my door with a translator. "They would like you to pray for them," the translator said.

"Are you pastors or evangelists?" I asked, hoping to better understand their needs.

They smiled and replied, "Yes."

"How many house churches do you oversee?" I inquired further.

The translator pointed to the woman on the left. "This one oversees 2,000 churches, and this other one oversees 5,000 churches," he said.

I was stunned. "Some denominations in the United States are still arguing about whether a woman can stand behind a pulpit," I said to myself. "Meanwhile, women in China are engaging in dangerous missions and governing thousands of new churches. There's something wrong with this picture!"

Since my trip to China I have met many other women who face incredible hardships as they engage in bold ministry. Like the female apostle Junia, who served alongside the apostle Paul and who was imprisoned with him (see Romans 16:7), these women are willing to die for Christ.

One of these modem Junias is Natasha Shedrevaya, a Russian

church planter who oversees 30 churches in Russia and 300 churches in the former republics of the Soviet Union. Her goal is to plant a church in every village in the Siberian north, a region spanning several time zones where most people have never heard the gospel.

I met another modern Junia about 15 years ago when Kayy Gordon visited my office. Gordon spent 40 years in the far north of Canada, reaching the isolated Inuit people, sometimes called Eskimos. Never married, this dedicated woman obeyed God's call and went to live in a desolate place most people would never dare visit.

Gordon had to travel from village to village by dog sled during the first years of her difficult ministry. Later, after more workers joined her team, she lost one of her best staff members in a plane crash. Yet even the most discouraging circumstances did not take Gordon off the front lines. At the time she retired, she had planted 12 churches and founded two Bible colleges. The seeds she planted in the Arctic tundra produced a spiritual awakening throughout that region.

Amazingly, when I share stories of women like Kayy Gordon, Natasha Shedrevaya, or the brave Chinese women, some people still object. They say, "I don't think women can be leaders," or "God wants men to be the initiators, not women."

How ridiculous! The Bible calls all believers—not just men—to be bold witnesses. And the Scriptures do not suggest that only men can initiate. All of us should display the kind of overcoming faith that drives us to surmount obstacles, believe for miracles, trample on devils, and challenge the status quo.

This is why I was so thrilled when I learned of Jamie Morgan's ministry. Jamie is one of these brave apostolic women leaders who have been raised up by God for this hour. As a man, I'm not threatened by Jamie's anointing to teach or preach—I am edified.

I'm not worried about her assuming spiritual authority—because she wears the mantle well, and she walks in divine grace.

I am especially thrilled that Jamie is challenging women all over the world to bravely step into their spiritual callings, no matter what their detractors say. That is the purpose of this book, *Her Calling*. I believe this book will throw more fuel on the fire of the Holy Spirit that already burns in the hearts of women who are called to ministry.

Jamie Morgan reminds me of Catherine Booth, who found herself in the middle of this controversy more than 150 years ago. Booth co-founded the Salvation Army with her husband, William, in 1865. At that time many staunch critics of women preachers were telling her that it was "unfeminine" for her to preach the gospel. So in 1859 she wrote a pamphlet, *Female Teaching: Women's Right to Preach the Gospel*.

Booth's writing is still one of the clearest defenses of a woman's right to preach ever penned. Yet her critics continued to throw tomatoes and apples at her when she spoke on street corners in London while wearing her signature black bonnet.

Not only did she eloquently dissect the words of the apostle Paul to prove that he had women preachers on his team (such as Priscilla, Phoebe, Euodia, Syntyche, and others), but Booth asked a powerful question: "If God were against women preachers, why does it seem the Holy Spirit is blessing the ministry of women who speak publicly?"

Catherine Booth's critics dismissed her. But her legacy is legendary. Booth often quoted Acts 2:17, which says, *"'In the last days it shall be,' says God, 'that I will pour out My Spirit on all flesh; your sons and your daughters shall prophesy'"* (Acts 2:17a MEV). For Mrs. Booth, this was the Emancipation Proclamation for women in the church. It clearly states that women will speak for God after the coming of the Holy Spirit's power.

What does *"your daughters shall prophesy"* mean if it doesn't mean they will preach? Does it mean they can preach only on street corners outside the church? Does it mean they are only sanctioned to conduct Bible studies for women? Does it mean they can preach as long as they don't stand behind a Plexiglas pulpit? Does it mean they can preach as long as there are no "adult men" in the audience?

I don't believe Peter's sermon in Acts 2 was about limitation. I don't think Acts 2:17 contains an asterisk with a footnote in small print that says, "*Only in certain situations." Acts 2:17 is about freedom. Pentecost removed the gender barrier. When the flames of Pentecost came upon the early disciples, the fire was not blue for the men and pink for the women! It was the same holy fire resting on everyone!

Our manmade restrictions are so silly. If God has said, "Your daughters shall prophesy," why are we so afraid of giving anointed women a platform? I've been defending women's rights to preach for 30 years, and I'm convinced it is the devil who is working overtime to keep Spirit-filled women out of the pulpit. Satan is terrified of what will happen when women called by God are released to fully obey that calling.

Thank you, Jamie Morgan, for your example to the body of Christ. Thank you for stirring the embers of revival with this important book. My prayer is that *Her Calling* will ignite a fresh flame in the hearts of God's daughters, and that an army of anointed women will step into their places as pastors, teachers, prophets, evangelists, and apostolic leaders for this new generation.

—J. Lee Grady, author of *10 Lies the Church Tells Women*
Director of The Mordecai Project
Former Editor of Charisma Magazine

TABLE OF CONTENTS

INTRODUCTION

One morning while I was sitting at the feet of Jesus, I asked Him to give me His heart. I pray this often when I have my daily devotions, but on that particular day God answered me in a dramatic way. In a vision, He pulled back a curtain to reveal to me His heart. And when He did, what I saw was the most luscious, thick, beautiful field that was ready for harvest that I had ever seen. It seemed to go on forever, as far as the eye could see.

But God wasn't finished. As the vision continued, He zoomed in the view to give me a much closer look. Intermittently spaced within the harvest field I saw a number of round, black circles and knew they were placeholders. They were the size of a base used in baseball and represented places where harvesters should be standing but were not.

And then I heard the Lord say,

> The harvest is great, but the workers are few [Matthew 9:37]. In this hour I need both male *and female* laborers to take their places in the last days' harvest of souls. I am calling you to identify, gather, and mobilize the female laborers to arise in their particular areas of ministry specialization and bring in the harvest. There is a place in the harvest field of souls awaiting every woman of God.

I wrote this book in response to God's call on my life. And I wrote it to equip you to answer God's call on yours. Whether your calling is behind the pulpit, behind the cubicle at work, behind the doors of your church, or behind the front door of your home, the Lord is calling you to ARISE and take your place in the harvest field that He has been holding just for you.

Sadly, most women aren't walking in their calling. And even those who do are usually walking in only partial fulfillment of their callings. Why? The reasons are many and varied—lack of confidence, lack of training, lack of resources, lack of knowledge, lack of encouragement, lack of inspiration, lack of support, and yes, all too often lack of a mentor.

I wrote this book for women with a calling, and that includes YOU. You have a calling on your life. Your gifts and talents are just waiting to bloom! But you need a mentor to walk alongside you to help you fulfill your God-given purpose in life.

And I want to be your mentor.

The pages of this book contain a lifetime of wisdom, experience, and direction from the trenches of ministry. It's my honor to impart to you all the Lord has given to me so you can stand on my shoulders and advance the Kingdom.

Part of my goal in writing *Her Calling: A Woman's Guide to Fulfilling Her God-given Destiny* is for it to become a mentor in a book—addressing the spiritual and practical questions that women in training desperately want to know but have no one to ask. If I mentored you for five years, the words in this book are what I would say to you.

This book is for women who can identify with one or more of the following statements.

- I know what I'm called to do but don't know how to start.
- I need help determining my specific calling.
- I've let distractions get in the way of my calling.
- I've resisted my calling.
- I could be more fruitful and productive in my calling.
- I need help articulating my calling.
- I have wounds that need healing.

- I do the work of ministry without the title.
- I dream of being in the ministry one day.
- I'm called to the Ephesians 4:11 five-fold ministry.
- I'm a pastor's wife.
- I'm in Bible college training for the ministry.
- I'm in the ministry and need a mentor.
- I'm in the ministry, have a mentor, but need another voice speaking into my life.
- I'm in the ministry and need help navigating the ministry ropes of being a woman in ministry.
- I attend a church that doesn't believe in women in ministry and desperately need support.
- I'm so discouraged that I'm ready to quit the ministry.

I intend this book to be a catalyst in the hands of Almighty God to catapult you into His destiny for your life. You may read it from front to back cover, or you may use it as a reference book, but my recommendation is for you to do both. As you're reading, ask God to breathe the wind of His Spirit through the pages of this book to awaken your heart and set you on fire to answer His call on your life.

Woman of God, there's a *placeholder* in God's ripe harvest field with your name on it.

Will you do what it takes to answer God's call? There's a lost and dying world that awaits your answer.

Let's go! Let's GO! LET'S GO!

—Jamie Morgan

CHAPTER 1

Your Time is Now

LET'S START THIS first chapter with a question. Who are you?

Trailblazer
Revivalist
Reformer
Forerunner
Fire Starter
Soul Winner
Disciple Maker
World Changer
History Maker
Nations' Shaker
Unstoppable Force
Christ's Ambassador
Minister of the Gospel

Woman of God, all of the above is who you are! I want you to pause for a moment and hold each of these in your heart as we begin preparing you for what God is calling you to do.

What an amazing journey awaits you! There's absolutely nothing in the entire world that compares to answering God's call on your life—*nothing*. The riches of this world, the vacation of your dreams, the most extravagant mansion, a private jet—nothing the world has to offer comes even a close second to walking in your calling, purpose, and destiny. And that's because this is what we were placed on earth to do.

You were not drawn to this book by chance. God wants to use you to change the world for Jesus Christ. And now is the time for you to answer His call on your life with no reservation!

A LITTLE ABOUT ME

I'm an ordained minister who has been in the ministry for decades. I've been a senior pastor, evangelist, teacher of the Word, revivalist, reformer, a prophetic voice, an apostolic Kingdom leader, prayer warrior, missionary, conference speaker, podcaster, TV show host, author, and mentor. And I've served at the local church level in every imaginable capacity. (But the sound booth . . . please don't make me serve in the sound booth! Ha ha.) I don't list these things to brag, only to relate. I've probably already stood where God is about to promote you.

I've also experienced almost every conceivable ministry pain in addition to mountain-top victories. And in retrospect, I'm utterly grateful for all I've gone through—the good, bad, and ugly—so I can help you in your journey. Jesus is worth it all! And I assure you, *you* are worth *everything* to Jesus.

As my ministry matured, I began inspiring, encouraging, and challenging women called to the ministry to walk in every ounce of their calling, mantle, and anointing. I began helping women navigate the ropes of being a woman in ministry. (Only another woman in ministry can fully mentor you through that.)

Then God instructed me to launch the Trailblazer Mentoring Network (TrailblazerMentoring.com)—a mentoring movement for women called to ministry.

And now through that ministry and this book, I get to be *YOUR* mentor!

My present assignment from God is to mentor women of God who recognize their need for a mentor in order to walk in the FULLNESS of their callings. *Partial* fulfillment of your calling will never do.

I am exceedingly passionate about helping you discover your calling, step out in faith, and blast through every obstacle and stronghold that the enemy sends your way! And as always, my overarching purpose for doing that is *souls*—to see a vast harvest of souls come into the Kingdom through whatever area of specialized ministry God has assigned to you.

I'm so honored to be your mentor. It's truly a privilege to walk beside you through the pages of this book as you follow hard after Jesus and His call on your life. To God be the glory for the great things He is going to do!

I'M SO VERY SORRY

You may be included in the vast multitude of women called to ministry who've yet to answer God's call due to general lack of support or even a never-ending barrage of opposition. Or you may be counted among the immeasurable number of women who have answered God's call, but due to a shortage of mentors, you aren't at the level you know you could obtain. Perhaps you are treading water in the ministry and feel like at any moment you could sink.

Someone needs to acknowledge the hurt, pain, loneliness, and injustices you've withstood at the hand of the enemy. And let that someone be me. Woman of God, I can both understand and identify with your frustration.

I'm sorry if you've been discouraged in your calling. I'm sorry if you've been discounted or overlooked for ministry positions. I'm sorry if you've been made to feel like a leper at ministers' gatherings. I'm sorry if the expectations of those around you are low when it comes to what you can contribute. I'm sorry for every critical stone that has been hurled your way. I'm sorry for every time you heard a speaker at ministers' gatherings address the ministers in the room as "you boys," "you men," or "you guys."

I'm also sorry that entire church doctrines have been written to preclude you from ministry. I'm sorry if you've been taught that women are God's fallback option if a man isn't willing or available. I'm sorry if you've been barred from physically standing behind a pulpit. (Yes, this has happened to me.)

I'm so sorry if you've heard altar calls for vocational ministry addressed only to men. I'm sorry if anyone has ever labeled you a Jezebel. I'm sorry if you've been called the "B" word for exhibiting strong leadership gifts (even if the word only crossed their minds). I'm sorry for all the times you had to stop advancing the Kingdom in order to answer your critics.

I'm deeply sorry for the dissatisfaction you've felt in life for not walking in your purpose. I'm sorry if you've endured the pain of rejection and loneliness. I'm sorry if your gifts and talents have lain dormant.

I'm also sorry if you've rarely, if ever, seen a woman modeling spiritual leadership in your church or denomination. I'm sorry for all the wasted time. I'm sorry if needed ministry support has been sorely lacking. I'm sorry if no one pours encouragement and wisdom into you. I'm sorry if you've had to encourage yourself in the Lord again and again out of necessity.

I'm sorry if no one has cared enough to check your ministry pulse. I'm sorry if you have no one whom you can ask practical ministry questions. I'm sorry you've had to navigate major ministry problems alone. I'm sorry if you haven't had a mentor. I'm so very sorry.

How do I know what you've endured? I can identify with everything I've expressed above and more. While this isn't a let-me-tell-you-everything-they-did-to-me list, someone needs to call out these things somewhere along the line and let you know she cares. It brings healing, and it will help propel you forward into your ministry destiny.

It's important to note that my apology doesn't come from a feeling of victimization (more on this later). You're a VICTOR no matter the hardships you've undergone.

Nonetheless, the pain you've withstood is real and needs to be recognized. As your mentor, I am honored to acknowledge what you've suffered—and I want to bring healing, encouragement, and guidance to you.

I'm sorry. I'm so very, very sorry. From the bottom of this female minister's heart, I'm genuinely sorry.

Forgive them, for they know not what they do.

I AFFIRM YOU

As your mentor, I affirm there is a calling on your life—a destiny God has called you to fulfill. I affirm that you're loaded with gifts, talents, anointings, and mantles. I affirm that you were born with a purpose to fulfill and that your very existence on this earth proves there is something God wants to accomplish through you.

I also affirm that there are people God has called you to reach with the gospel. I affirm that God will prepare, equip, and launch you into the place of ministry to which you've been called. I affirm that you are God's first choice for the ministry to which you are called—that you were hand-picked by Almighty God for that very purpose.

I affirm that you are anointed and appointed for such a time as this to fulfill the Great Commission. You've been given a mandate by God to present the gospel, lay hands on the sick, and cast out demons (regardless of your particular ministry assignment); all of which you'll do with great boldness and without succumbing to hindrances.

I affirm that your feet are beautiful (Romans 10:15). Your words will be filled with power when you speak. Your mind will be filled with wisdom. Your eyes will be fixed on Jesus, and you'll keep your hand on the plow.

I affirm that God will help you answer His call on your life. He will perform miracles, open doors, part rivers, and move mountains on your behalf. He will blast through every obstacle the enemy places in your path to hinder you from answering His call.

I affirm that you are a daughter of God upon whom He has poured His Spirit. God chooses whom He chooses, and He has chosen *you*!

Yes, you've been hurt, discouraged, and disappointed. But I end this section by affirming that He will use you to minister salvation, healing, and deliverance to the lost and broken. And He will use everything you've been through for your benefit. God is THAT good!

YOUR MENTORING SUCCESS PATH

Now grab my hand and let me walk you through what to expect in your mentoring experience. One step at a time, I will take you down the road of walking in the *fullness* of your calling using the following points of interest to map out our way.

First, I will help you identify your specific purpose by asking signpost questions that point to your ministry destiny. You'll discover your ministry assignment like a gold miner digs for gold. You'll also learn the dangers of comparing yourself to others, becoming a cookie-cutter minister, and not staying in your own ministry lane.

In addition, you'll understand that preparation is crucial to the success and fruitfulness of your future ministry. You will appreciate why Christ-like character, integrity, and establishing yourself in the Word and Spirit must take place before God can release you to your task. And just like a good farmer learns to cooperate with the seasons, you'll ascertain how to cooperate with God in every season of your ministry life.

I'll also help you realize that Satan has a plan to sabotage your destiny and expose areas where you have possible agreement with the enemy. I'll identify eight of the most common excuses that I've heard women called to ministry make for why they're not answering God's call. And I'll give you a seven-step plan to foil Satan's plan to stop God's purposes from coming to pass in your life.

You'll also learn how to articulate your calling, formulate a personal theology of women in ministry, and answer those who object to women in ministry. You'll be able to discern when to answer your critics and when to ignore them. And regardless of the support you receive, or lack thereof, you'll understand how to confidently carry yourself in the calling God has placed on your life.

Additionally, you'll discover the concept that intercessory prayer is to your ministry what the immune system is to the human body. You will learn the importance of spiritual warfare in your ministry and how to have victory when the enemy attacks. And you'll understand the importance of bathing every aspect of your ministry in prayer and surrounding yourself with a team of dedicated intercessors.

You'll also see the importance of having a mentor and being a good protégé. And you'll learn how to mentor those who are coming up behind you. You'll ascertain the character traits to look for in a mentor, how to find a mentor, how to ask someone to be your mentor, how to receive correction and critiques, and the value of accountability. And you'll obtain wisdom in choosing friends wisely and learn how godly friendships are essential for a healthy life and ministry.

Plus, you'll learn the practicalities of ministry, from how to hold a microphone to how to prepare a message. You'll be taught how to interpret and teach your audience by asking pertinent questions and how to organize future message topics so you are ready when God opens the door. Moreover, you'll learn topics such as ministry manners, honoring the rules of the house, and staying within time constraints .

We'll also examine topics unique to traveling ministers, such as scheduling services, accepting invitations, and receiving love offerings versus an honorarium. You'll become well versed in subjects like product sales, the importance of knowing the doctrines of the church/ministry you are visiting, and how to use wisdom when traveling alone. And I'll help you determine the host's expectations for the event and how to communicate your expectations to the host as well.

You'll also learn how to expect the supernatural power of God to flow through you by staying in unbroken fellowship with the person of the Holy Spirit. You'll be able to discern between the three categories of the anointing of God. You'll recognize the purposes of the anointing and understand anointings unique to you. You will also gain a better grasp of what hinders the anointing.

Along with that, you'll come to understand that in addition to the joy of ministry, there is pain. You'll be taught how to gain victory over the most common wounds in ministry. You'll also be taught to cultivate a soft heart, to have skin like Teflon, and to know there is purpose in the pain. And you'll also see that looking more like Jesus is your ultimate goal.

Furthermore, you'll learn how to stay the course and take the word *quit* out of your vocabulary. You'll understand the correlation between our pain threshold and ministry longevity and success. You'll see why placing healthy boundaries around your God-given assignment, maintaining your joy, and walking in love will help determine the vitality of your ministry. And you'll learn the secret sauce of ministers—the personal retreat.

And lastly, you'll understand the indescribable rewards of ministry. You'll discover that God is a rewarder and see the types of rewards He gives. And you'll realize that Jesus is our ultimate reward here on earth as well as in Heaven. And that means, no matter what we must endure to answer our callings, Jesus is worth it all.

THE URGENCY OF THE HOUR

There is a spiritual urgency in the air, an eternal clock ticking in the background. The lost and hurting are waiting for you to answer God's unique call on your life. Souls are hanging in the balance. Wasted time is a thing of the past; excuses will no longer suffice. Remember, Satan dines on what you withhold from God. Stop saying, "If only things were different I would . . . ." It's time for utter obedience and death to self.

Jesus said to His disciples,

> *If any of you wants to be my follower, you must give up your own way, take up your cross, and follow me. If you try to hang on to your life, you will lose it. But if you give up your life for my sake, you will save it. And what do you benefit if you gain the whole world but lose your own soul? Is anything worth more than your soul?* (Matthew 16:24-26)[1]

But what does it mean to *save your life*?

For those not willing to lose their lives to follow Jesus, saving your life is having the attitude that you want to keep your life intact. In other words it's like saying,

> "I like my little life just the way it is, thank you very much. I want to stay comfortable and protect my feelings. I want to

1 Unless otherwise annotated, Scripture references are taken from the New Living Translation, copyright © 1996, 2004, 2015 by Tyndale House Foundation. Used by permission of Tyndale House Publishers, Inc., Carol Stream, Illinois 60188.

> keep myself from anything that would drain me. I want to control my own life.
>
> "I want to *give out* only when it suits me, so that at the end of my life I will have lived a safe, smooth, sanitary, dignified, unstrained, and untattered life. Then, when that time comes, I'll be able to say that I've never been burned out, used up, or bent over from carrying too heavy a load. And I've avoided being laughed at, mocked, rejected, scorned, assaulted, or falsely accused."

Come on, now. Let's rip off the rearview mirror and stop making excuses. Come to the place where you realize disobedience is not an option. Own the fact that living in your comfort zone is akin to dying in the graveyard of your calling. With every assignment from God there will be opposition from the enemy. You can count on it!

Paul wrote in 1 Corinthians 16:9, *"There is a wide-open door for a great work here, although many oppose me."* Attacks are distractions to take our focus off of the work God has given us to do. If we give our attention to the enemy, our eyes are no longer on God's call. We must look past the distractions the enemy has placed before us and walk—*no, run!*—through those ministry doors God has opened.

Nehemiah is a great example of how to handle distractions that come to derail God's call. He was assigned to rebuild the wall around Jerusalem. While doing that, his enemies decided they wanted to have a meeting with him. Nehemiah discerned it was a trap to wear him down, get him off course, and stop the advancement of God's work.

So Nehemiah made one of the most important decisions in the rebuilding process. He sent a courier to them with this message: *"I am engaged in a great work, so I can't come. Why should I stop working to come and meet with you?"* (Nehemiah 6:3).

When trials come, the temptation is to stop doing what God has called you to do. But like Nehemiah, you need to make God's call on your life your first concern. Jesus' command to *"Go and make disciples . . ."* (Matthew 28:19) needs to be your first priority.

The things of this world can also be a distraction seducing you and deterring you from fulfilling your destiny in God. If the devil can get you to worship the things of this world instead of Almighty God, your response to God's call will get derailed. And it usually comes in the form of compromise.

Remember reading in Luke about Satan tempting Jesus in the wilderness? The devil took Jesus on top of a mountain and showed Him all the kingdoms of this world.

> *"I will give you the glory of these kingdoms and authority over them," the devil said, "because they are mine to give anyone I please. I will give it all to you if you will worship me."*
>
> (Luke 4:6–7)

Satan unsuccessfully tried to tempt Jesus with compromise. Satan's goal was to get Jesus to bypass the cross—get Him to abandon His ultimate purpose in coming to earth. You better believe the enemy will tempt you with worldly distractions to thwart your calling. He tempted Jesus, and he'll tempt you too.

Your response to the enemy when he tries to dangle bright shiny objects before you to distract you from building the Kingdom needs to be that of Jesus.

> *The Scriptures say, "You must worship the Lord your God and serve only Him."* (Luke 4:8)

So say this with me:

Get behind me, Satan, because I WILL FULFILL GOD'S CALL ON MY LIFE!

With every new door comes new challenges and threats, but the Lord will cause a strength to rise within you that will bring completion of His assignment on your life. However, you must keep your eyes on your purpose, letting nothing distract you.

I assure you, God will use the pain you've endured to help you. The biggest black eye you can give the devil is to take from him that which he tried to kill, steal, and destroy and allow God to turn it around, restore you, and bring salvation and healing to others.

Every day when you wake up you'll have taken ground from the devil, or he'll have taken ground from you. It's your decision which one will happen, and your own spiritual success or failure will depend largely on where you put your attention. Keep your attention on God and the work He has called you to do, and you'll find success.

The nations of the world are at a tipping point. We're experiencing spiritual warfare on every level and on all fronts. The Church is lukewarm and too often asleep. Many leave their Sunday morning services with nothing more than a coffee buzz from the café in the lobby. The Holy Spirit wants to jolt us awake with His power! Are you willing to move into your calling and deliver this message to the world around you?

God is searching the whole earth for women who will do great exploits for Him, advance the Kingdom, and set the world on fire for the Lord Jesus Christ. He is conducting the most aggressive pursuit in the history of humankind to find that one who will say YES!

It's time to lose your life for Christ, count the cost, and risk it all.

Your time is NOW!

CHAPTER 2

Identifying Your Calling

I
HATE
REGRETS.

I mean I *really* hate regrets. I endeavor to live my life with as few regrets as possible. Oh, like everyone else, I have a slew of them, but there's one regret I absolutely refuse to have. And here it is:

To have died without having fulfilled God's purposes for my life.

I won't miss out on hearing my Savior say, "Well done, good and faithful servant." Hearing that divine declaration will imply I did what God asked me to do, did it well, did it with a servant's heart, and was faithful while doing it. Not hearing those words would be the ultimate regret. This future encounter with Jesus compels me to find my calling, and it continues to drive me to fulfill every ounce of it!

And I want to help you do the same.

But first, congratulations are in order! You already know you are called by God to do great things for Him. If I could give you a high five or fist bump, I would! That's way more than most Christians comprehend about their lives. But now—what *are* you called to do for God? Practically speaking, how do you determine the specifics of your calling? I struggled with this for many years. I've coined this season of the ministry journey the *Pregnancy Stage* of ministry.

Perhaps this is the place where you are now.

In the Pregnancy Stage of ministry you're pregnant with the call of God but aren't showing. You don't look pregnant. That was me. From outward appearances, I didn't look like someone God could use in ministry. There was little evidence of His call on my life. I didn't look like ministry material to the people around me, or even to myself.

I had just gotten saved and was fresh off the alcoholism, panic attack, and depression truck. When Jesus rescued me from the pit, I was twenty-six years old—serving up to myself cocktails of Xanax and alcohol—and a prisoner in my home due to anxiety attacks. My entire world was limited to my bed. Many times when my husband left for work, I was in bed with the covers pulled up over my head only to have him return in the evening to find me still in the same location.

Rinse and repeat: Although I was saved, I didn't look like ministry material.

David was a young shepherd tending his father's flock and was discounted for ministry as God's anointed King of Israel. Perhaps David was viewed as too young, or he didn't look "kingly" enough. Although people had discounted me unsuitable for the ministry because of my past, God didn't.

> *The Lord doesn't see the things the way you see them. People judge by outward appearance, but the Lord looks at the heart.*
>
> (1 Samuel 16:7b)

I'm so glad God chooses whom He chooses; aren't you?

So there I was, pregnant with the call of God, knowing I was going to give birth to a ministry, but I didn't have a clue about when it would happen or what that bundle-of-joy was going to look like. So I began the most important quest I've ever undertaken—to find God's purposes for my life.

See, here's the thing: God created you for a specific purpose. Your purpose is deep down inside of you. Most Christians will die never having fulfilled their callings. Even those who know what God has called them to do will all too often let the distractions, discouragements, and setbacks we all experience in life keep them from fulfilling their destinies in God.

We must not fail to both realize and fulfill the destinies God planned for us. It's our job to seek God for our purposes and to do them *well*.

LET NOTHING STOP YOU!

So if you're at this point, let me walk beside you and give you six crucial steps to uncover your calling, purpose, and destiny in God. While this isn't a formula, it will put you on the right spiritual track for God to reveal His plans for your life.

STEP ONE: FORGET THE PAST

This might seem like an odd first step, but without it you won't press into God for your destiny. The following Scripture contains two extremely important components to finding your purpose in life.

> *... but I focus on this one thing:* ***Forgetting the past*** *and looking forward to what lies ahead, I* ***press on*** *to reach the end of the race and receive the heavenly prize for which God, through Christ Jesus, is calling us.* (Philippians 3:13-14 emphasis mine)

Forgetting the past and pressing on—forget and press on. Forget and press on!

Before we press on to discover God's plans for us, we must forget what's behind. If we don't forget the past, we won't fully run the race God has designed for our lives and receive the heavenly prize for answering our calling. If we don't forget the past, even if we answer God's call, we will limp through the race instead of running with reckless abandon!

We all have a past. We could all write a book (especially me) on our mistakes, flops, washouts, mess-ups, botches, duds, and failures. We've all started projects we didn't finish, wasted time and money, said things we shouldn't have said, done things we shouldn't have done, and perhaps stepped out in faith with what we thought was a *God* idea only to discover it was just a *good* idea (or bad idea as the case may be). And we've all sinned and fallen short of the glory of God.

Ladies, we have an enemy who doesn't want us to answer God's call. And he will use our past to condemn us so we won't say "YES" to God. He will hammer us with all we've done wrong and all the reasons we shouldn't move forward in God's plans for our lives. And then he will put the hammer in our hands to have us finish ourselves off.

Sometimes holding on to the past can be a safety net, because even if it's bad, it's familiar—like a demonic security blanket. We need to let go of the safety net called "the past" and secure ourselves in Jesus. Others build a monument to the past that's specific to something they did or what was done to them. They pitch a tent at the monument stone they constructed and pay homage to it by giving it a place in their thought life. In essence, they worship it. If that's you, *STOP IT!!!*

Forget what's behind. Fix your eyes on Jesus and press on. Press on for all those to whom you'll minister. Press on for those who come behind you. Press on for your children and grandchildren (both natural and spiritual). Press on for the lost souls destined for hell. And most importantly, press on because Jesus is worthy of your effort.

STEP TWO: ASK GOD

Prayer is the beginning, middle, and end of seeking God for His assignment on your life. But here is the key. Your prayers must be persistent, intentional, and specific. The polar opposite is praying sporadically, casually, and generally. You need to pray for God to unveil your destiny like it's your main priority. Pray for God to show you His assignment on your life like someone's eternity depends on it, because it does.

Here is a sample prayer model to incorporate into your daily time with the Lord. These prayer points will help steer you in the right direction to seek God regarding your calling and act as launching pads to lead you to additional Spirit-led supplication. I refer to them as the Seven A's of Purpose.

The Seven A's of Purpose

- *Assignment*—"Lord, what am I called to accomplish?"
- *Area*—"Lord, where am I called to accomplish it?"
- *Authority*—"Lord, reveal my sphere of influence."
- *Alignment*—"Lord, align my life with the relationships required to fulfill my calling."
- *Accuracy*—"Lord, give me accuracy in what I am called to accomplish for maximum ministry effectiveness."
- *Abundance*—"Lord, give me a vast harvest of souls and fruit that remains."
- *Anointing*—"Lord, anoint me mightily for what you've called me to accomplish."

Praying the Seven A's of Purpose can prove foundational to

you fulfilling your calling as you press into it through prayer. Let them act as a starting point as you begin to press into God with everything in you regarding God's plan for your ministry life.

STEP THREE: START SERVING IN YOUR LOCAL CHURCH—*ANYWHERE NEEDED*

An essential element in discovering my calling was through serving in my local church. God's growth plan for the believer is housed in the local church. If my pastor asked me to make phone calls, I placed calls like I was calling Jesus. If the pastor's wife needed my help cleaning the church, I swept the floors like I was sweeping the streets of gold. And if the nursery needed snacks, I baked cookies like Jesus was going to eat them. (And I'm not an enthusiastic baker!)

As I served in so many ways (some of them mundane), my gifts and talents began to emerge like signposts pointing in the direction of God's ordained destiny for my life. But even more importantly, God was cultivating within me a heart to serve. And my service was teaching me how to die to self and developing within me the character of Christ needed for full-time ministry.

By the way, and this is crucial to note, I didn't tell my pastor where I wanted to serve. Not that there's anything wrong with that, but I didn't do it. Rather, I asked him which ministries had the greatest need for workers.

See, it wasn't about me. It never is. It was all about fulfilling God's vision for my local church. Also, pastors don't just pastor their people. They also pastor their people's gifts. Most of the time, my pastor placed me in ministries that weren't in my "wheel house" or "skill set."

Here is one of my favorite passages in the book of Nehemiah: *"Next was Uzziel son of Harhaiah, a goldsmith by trade, who also worked on the wall. Beyond him was Hananiah, a manufacturer of perfumes"* (Nehemiah 3:8). The goldsmith and the perfume maker could have haughtily proclaimed, "Ugh, sorry, we're not masons. We only work with fine gold and choice spices and oils, not stones!" Instead, they were God's people and did what needed to be done. Period.

So for example, I'm not gifted to minister to children, but when I was asked to teach children's church, I threw myself into the task. And I didn't slap the lesson together at the last minute, either. Rather, I prepared the lesson like I was asked to speak to an audience of a thousand adults. I prayed for the handful of children to whom I would be ministering—like their souls were hanging in the balance between heaven and hell and it would be the only time they would ever hear the gospel.

Here's the thing. God watches to see what we do with what He has given us, especially when we're not serving in our "first choice" ministry. Will we take it seriously? Will we exhibit faithfulness and commitment? Will we view the people to whom we are ministering through the eyes of God?

God will only give us *much* ***IF*** we are faithful with what we consider *little*.

God will use those *out-of-our-gifting* serving opportunities to teach us how to 100% rely on the Lord. See, when we're serving in our ministry lane, there's a temptation to rely solely on our gifting. This is dangerous. Flesh begets flesh, Spirit begets Spirit (John 3:6).

When we aren't gifted to minister in a certain area, it forces us to pray, "Jesus, if you don't show up, the job won't get done. Please minister through me." This is the place God wants us to be—and the place He wants us to stay.

Blessed are those who completely and totally rely on God for absolutely everything, including ministry.

The other thing accomplished by serving anywhere asked is that it shows us what we are *not* called to do. A rock that's rolling is easier to move and direct than a boulder that's stationary. We have to get up and get moving in order for God to change our direction. He's not going to reveal your calling to you while you sit binge-watching a television show with a tub of popcorn in one hand and the remote control in the other. No, it's while you are serving when you'll discover a particular ministry is either "right up your alley" or, the converse, "not your cup of tea."

Eventually, as a result of faithfully serving in areas I would never have chosen, God began opening doors of ministry in areas where I was called. As I conducted a women's midweek Bible study, my teaching and preaching gifts emerged. As I hosted a life group, shepherding gifts surfaced. As I spearheaded church outreaches, my calling as evangelist developed. And as I led other ministries, various other leadership gifts began to appear. God used all of those ministry experiences to reveal my calling, one day at a time, as I continued to faithfully and consistently put my hand to the ministry plow.

STEP FOUR: IDENTIFY YOUR PASSIONS

God often gives us glimpses or signposts pointing to our callings directly related to the passions that He has woven into our DNA. Identifying and locating our passions will help us head in the direction of our purpose. Ask yourself the following passion questions to help you further define God's call on your life.

What do I love to do?

Often what you love to do will help reveal your purpose in life. What you do well differentiates you from others and represents your uniqueness. Make a list of all of your gifts and talents. Add to that list the ministry activities that bring you energy and make you feel the most alive. Walking inside your calling will be life-giving. Walking outside of your calling will deplete you.

And lastly, think back to childhood. What gifts and talents began emerging in you even as a youngster? When I was a little girl, I came home from school every day and taught my cat Sheba everything I learned in school that day. (She was the smartest cat in the world!) I know that almost every little girl at some point in her childhood wants to be a teacher, but I did that for *years* and *years*. Looking back, a strong teaching gift began to emerge in me even in my early elementary years.

What did you love to do as a little girl? Add these to your list as well.

Think back to all the times and areas in which you have served, both in sacred and secular work, and make a list of all of the gifts and talents that have surfaced over the years. Then ask those closest to you—people who have your best interest at heart—what gifts and talents they see in you. Add these to the list as well. Often people can see in us what we can't see in ourselves.

Here's another good question to ask yourself in order to drill down into your purpose: If every job on the face of the earth paid $10 per hour, from trash collector to world leader, what would you do for a living? What would you do if money were no issue and all limits were off? Add this to your list of what you love to do.

What makes me angry?

Anger is passion that can be a signpost of something you are called to correct. A biblical example of righteous anger is when Jesus overturned the moneychangers' tables in the temple (John 2:13-16). Jesus confronted what He was called to correct—the religious rulers who were leading people astray.

Our anger can awaken the mantle God placed on our lives to bring correction or resolution to a problem on this earth. Do you hate when things are unorganized or sloppy? Perhaps God has given you an administrative gifting. Do you hate divorce? Possibly God has called you to help troubled marriages. Do you hate abortion? Maybe God has called you to volunteer at your local pro-life pregnancy center or to plead the case of the unborn before lawmakers.

What make me angry is when Christians don't care about their purpose. I don't mean people who haven't identified their purpose but those who are apathetic about it. I can't stand the thought that there are people who wander aimlessly through life never having fulfilled their purpose *and don't care*! This points to a huge signpost that displays what I'm called to correct—help Christians understand they have a purpose and then assist them in finding it. Make a separate list of your anger signposts. (These lists will all make sense in a few pages.)

What makes me cry?

Sorrow can reveal what we are called to heal. What saddens or grieves us can give us a peek into our purpose. There are things that upset all of us (tragedies, atrocities, terrible things we read about in the news), but I'm talking about what *really, really, really* grieves us—repeatedly.

Domestic violence? Poverty? Sexual abuse of children? Disease? Drug Addiction? Racism? What pains you to the point that, when others can walk right by a problem, you have to stop and get involved—you must get involved? What makes me cry is the thought of someone spending eternity in hell. This indicates that I not only have an evangelistic calling on my life (which is actually the calling of every Christian), but taking it one step further, I have a calling to impart my passion for souls into others as an evangelist. Make another list of things that grieve you to the point of action.

Who Do I Love?

The people we love can also be indicators of our callings. First and foremost, your family is your primary ministry. Some Christians want to be used in a *great* way when their ministry is sitting around their breakfast table. However, knowing our families are our first ministries is no excuse for not fulfilling God's other assignments on our lives.

Do you have a heart for youth? Perhaps you are called to youth ministry. Do you have a burden for a people in a particular region or nation? Maybe you are called to minister to that group of people. Do you feel deeply connected to the elderly? Possibly you are called to nursing home ministry.

One of the people groups for which I have a great burden is women called to the ministry who have little to no support. This passion drove me to launch *Trailblazer Mentoring Network* and write this book. Make another list consisting of individuals and groups you love and for whom you feel a burden to help.

STEP FIVE: RECALL YOUR GOD ENCOUNTERS

How has God already encountered you regarding His call on your life? It's time to get out your Bibles with notes written in the margins and your prayer journals filled with your relationship-moments with God. Reflect on the times God has already spoken to you regarding His assignment on your life. The Holy Spirit has as many ways to encounter us with our callings as there are grains of sand on the beach. He can encounter us through,

- Dreams.
- Visions.
- His still small voice.
- His audible voice.

- A Rhema Word of God (illuminated Scripture).
- Revelation knowledge.
- Your pastor's guidance.
- The voice and counsel of others.
- Seeming coincidences.
- Divine appointments.
- Open doors.
- Closed doors.
- Prophecies.
- A sudden memory that comes to mind.
- A knowing in your knower.
- Impressions.
- A miraculous sign or wonder.
- Peace in your spirit.
- A check in your spirit.

Ask the Lord to dust off encounters you've experienced to bring them back to your remembrance. Make a list of those things God used to either hint at your calling or give you blatant direction regarding His purposes for your life.

STEP SIX: CREATE A PURPOSE TIMELINE

This step is where it all comes together. *Warning*: there will be a temptation to skip this step, but please don't. It's well worth the effort. Creating a purpose timeline will help you visually see all glimpses that God has given you regarding His call on your life.

We need to seek our callings like a gold miner digs for gold. Sometimes a miner will dig for a long time before the gold appears.

Pursuing our callings can require patience and faith. But when gold is discovered, the gold miner digs more excitedly as he follows the glimmer he sees on the wall of the mine shaft. God will typically give you a glimpse of your calling, and then another glimpse, and so on, until you find your calling and walk in the light He has given you.

At this stage it's also important to understand that some people receive their callings abruptly and dramatically, like Jeremiah or Ezekiel. Others, however, discover their ministry callings gradually and progressively. My calling to ministry came as a combination of both. I believe it happens that way for most.

This is the reason creating a purpose timeline is so crucial. It will help you see God's hand on your life, recall His words spoken to your heart, and gain clarity by putting all the God-glimpses together.

Here are the materials you'll need for your Purpose Timeline:

- *Post-it* notes in 6 different colors
- The largest white poster board you can find

Following is how I created my own Purpose Timeline. (Note: It doesn't matter the color of *Post-it* notes, but for illustrative purposes I will share the colors I used.)

- I wrote down my identified gifts and talents, individually, on yellow *Post-it* notes.
- What I love to do—green.
- What makes me angry—orange.
- What makes me cry—pink.
- Who I love—purple.
- God encounters—blue.

Individually place each sticky note before you on a large table. You now have in front of you, via the *Post-it* notes, all the glimpses you've received over your lifetime. It probably looks like an incoherent jumble at this point. But wait! The Holy Spirit will bring it all together for you.

Now place the white poster board, horizontally, in front you and write across the top the various stages of your life. Write a minimum of three and a maximum of six stages in columnar fashion. The stages of your life can be anything you want them to be, but here are some examples:

- Ages (examples: birth-10, 11-21, 22-40, and so forth)
- Places you've lived (examples: Trenton, NJ; Levittown, PA; Millville, NJ)
- Roles in life (newlywed, young mother, mother to young adults, empty nester)
- Spiritual milestones (unsaved, new believer, healing years, etc.)

Please pause at this point. This is a holy moment. Ask the Holy Spirit to help you place each *Post-it* note under the stage/column that each particular calling-glimpse occurred. Begin placing the notes, one by one, under that stage of your life. After you've completed this step, here is the last and most important thing to do:

STEP SEVEN: ASK THE HOLY SPIRIT TO SHOW YOU GOD'S CALL ON YOUR LIFE.

Some of the ways the Holy Spirit will show you His call on your life is by,

- Exposing common threads you hadn't seen before.
- Helping you see the overarching theme of your life.

- Making sense of why you've gone through what you have.
- Giving you fresh eyes to see your life from His perspective.
- Answering questions that went unanswered before.
- Showing you the purpose that was behind the pain.
- Connecting dots between situations you hadn't correlated before.

The Holy Spirit may show you things in an instant or over a period of time. Many people have taken a personal prayer retreat to create their purpose timeline in order to give God more dedicated time and space to speak to them.

After you've completed your timeline, find a close friend or family member and explain to that person the details of your purpose timeline. The Holy Spirit will continue to work even as you are explaining it to others. And most definitely, make an appointment with your pastor to show him or her what God helped you to see during such a holy process.

God installs signposts along the paths of our lives to direct us on our journeys with Him. As you pay careful attention to them, not letting anything slip by unnoticed, I'm confident God will clarify your ministry destiny. I've certainly found it to be true personally.

Woman of God, as passionate as you are in discovering your calling, purpose, and destiny, I assure you, it ***IS*** God's good pleasure to reveal them to you!

CHAPTER 3

Your Preparation

WAITING IS SO difficult. I completely understand. But having patience and persevering through the time of your preparation before God launches you into your calling is critical. And preparation time is never lost time.

"When, God, when?"

"How, God, how?"

"When will You launch me into ministry?"

"How will it transpire?"

"God, how much longer do I have to wait?"

These are questions I took before the Lord over and over while I was in the waiting room of God's call on my life. You may be in God's waiting room right now. For me, the wait was so L-O-N-G! At times it felt like my calling would never come to pass.

It's a weird dichotomy. On one hand, we *think* we're ready to answer His call long before God *knows* we're ready.

"Do it, God! I'm so ready!"

But on the other hand, when God launches us into our life's purpose, we don't *feel* ready. We think we need to have all of our ducks in a row with all the "*T*s" crossed and "*I*s" dotted.

"Now, God? I'm not ready!"

But if we waited for all the tiny details to be worked out, we would never step out into the ministry. And sadly, this is why so many will never get around to answering their callings.

So it's not the actual waiting that should be our focus during our time of preparation. Our focus should be on what we ***do*** while we're waiting.

I live in the *Garden State*. Although New Jersey has many densely populated cities, it also has a lot of farmland. While farmers need vast knowledge to farm well, one of the most important things they must know is the season they're presently in. Good farmers don't try to plant in the winter, or harvest in the spring. They recognize the season, work within the confines of that season, and don't try to make the season something it's not.

When speaking of the seasons of our lives, the same should be true with us. When we're in the season of preparation, it's important for us to work within that season. But how do we do that? We cooperate with God as He prepares us for our destiny in Him.

We'll waste precious time *wishing* it was another season. And if we work against it, we'll lengthen the season of the preparation. Don't doubt it. God will accomplish much in the waiting room of our calling as we learn what to do while we wait.

As I said, preparation is never lost time. It's valuable! The season of waiting is crucial to the effectiveness and fruitfulness of your future ministry. Don't resist it or wish it away but instead, embrace it.

STAYING ON THE POTTER'S WHEEL

Years ago, I had the opportunity to visit a *clay college* where fledgling potters were taught how to create beautiful pottery masterpieces. I'm not creative by nature, but I love watching people who are. The reason for my visit to the clay college on that particular day was to receive a deeper revelation of what Isaiah said. *"And yet, O LORD, you are our Father. We are the clay and you are the potter. We are all formed by your hand"* (Isaiah 64:8).

After sharing my aim with the pottery instructor, he was kind enough to take me through each stage of pottery making.

There are so many parallels to our crucial seasons of preparation and the process of making pottery. See yourself in each phase. And be encouraged that the *Potter* knows exactly what He's doing as you're waiting to become a vessel the Master can use on the day He launches you into your ministry.

You are the *clay*. The Lord is the *Potter*.

God has been waiting for you. You make yourself available. Then He reaches down, picks you up, and carries you to the Potter's house. You say, "Yes, Lord! Do in me what you will. I say 'YES' to your will and to your way. Whatever it takes, no matter how painful, do it!"

While God is the Potter, you must cooperate with Him as He molds and shapes you during the preparation process. Resistance and unwillingness will slow or completely halt the lump of clay from becoming a completed vessel.

The Lord scoops you up with His mighty, nail scarred hands, reaches into the depths of your heart, and says, "I love you. Trust Me." He tenderly places you in the center of the Potter's wheel and begins to mold you with His strong but gentle hands.

He adds water, more water, and then more water. Clay can only be molded with water. The water represents the Word and prayer. The enemy will do everything he can to get you out of the Word and the presence of God in prayer. Every strong Christian you really admire has received a lot of water and a lot of molding.

The crafty enemy whispers in your ear, "Skip your devotional time sitting at the feet of Jesus. You deserve a break today. Besides, you have too much to do. The world can't possibly function without you if you spend an hour with Jesus."

It's in this stage when you learn that your daily, divine appointment with God is the single most important event of the day. You discover that your ministry to the Lord must come before your ministry to people. You realize that as you develop an intimate relationship with Jesus, your effectiveness in ministry will supernaturally come out of the overflow of your time spent with Him.

You stay on the wheel and commit to spending daily time with Jesus, letting no one and nothing get in your way.

THE PROCESS OF RIBBING

The Master places His hand down into the clay and pushes and stretches. God always works from the inside out, forming your inner man. He pulls everything out that doesn't look like what He is fashioning you into. Unforgiveness, jealousy, bitterness, greed, the flesh, rebellion, and pride are put to death. He breaks up the fallow ground of the hard places in your heart.

During this time of shaping and stretching you're once again tempted to take yourself off the wheel. It's painful. But people are like rubber bands. They can't be used unless they are stretched. Just when you think you can't endure any more, God gets out an instrument. It's the *ribbing* tool.

Now God is using people and circumstances as tools in His hands to lop off the rough edges of your character and form you into the character of Christ. He places you in situations that force you to keep your eyes on Jesus to walk on water and not sink. You learn to love your enemies, not take offense, persevere in difficulty, encourage yourself in the Lord, live with integrity, and war in the Spirit—all necessary to learn for ministry longevity.

God isn't looking for perfect vessels, rather imperfect vessels to mold into things of beauty. Our highest purpose in life and ministry is to reflect the image of Jesus. Therefore, the Lord chips away whatever isn't of Him. As women of God, we must allow the Lord to *rib* us. And often He uses suffering to do it. Suffering is part of the Christian walk.

God allows us to go through trials to do a deep, preparatory work in our lives. He turns around for good what the enemy means for harm. God brings us to a state of brokenness and then mends us so He can pour himself into empty vessels that will contain His Spirit. He needs to be able to trust us with His fire.

Recently, I happened upon the following entry in one of my prayer journals. I penned it during a season of brokenness in my life.

> I'm in pain and wandering the wilderness; the pain is more agonizing than I can bear. I can't seem to find my way out. I have a broken heart, and my bruises have bruises. This has affected my life in ways most will never know or understand. There have been many times in my life when I felt like my head was just barely above water; this time I feel like I'm drowning with only seconds left to live.

Although that period of my life was excruciatingly painful, there was purpose in the pain. Somewhere during that trial, my focus shifted. Instead of staring straight at the pain of my throbbing heart, I lifted my eyes to see the loving hands of the Sculptor at work.

God doesn't waste pain.

SHAPED FOR YOUR PURPOSE

You're growing. It's a time of great favor and blessing as you begin to take shape. God has a purpose for every piece of clay, be it for a flowerpot, dish, vase, saltshaker, or pitcher. You can tell He's forming you as a Kingdom leader, but you were hoping your ministry would resemble the ministry of so-and-so's.

You've always wanted to be like her. Not happy with the vessel God has chosen you to be, you think to yourself, "Why can't I be pretty like other pieces of pottery I've seen?"

Pottery comes in different sizes, shapes, and colors, but in the end, it's all just clay. We each have different talents, giftings, ministries, and purposes. We can't wish we had someone else's mantle. We also can't judge the other pots. What if the prettier pots looked down on the plainer pots? Or the little pots were jealous of the big pots? Or they all talked about the pots that aren't yet finished?

Becoming content with God's call on our lives is part of the season of preparation. God doesn't make cookie-cutter ministers. We're all different, with vastly different calls on our lives. Own your calling. Relish it. Love it. *"Yet true godliness with contentment is itself great wealth"* (1 Timothy 6:6).

THE DRYING SHELF

Just when you were getting comfortable on the wheel, the Lord takes the Holy Spirit wire, cuts you off the wheel, and places you on the shelf to dry. What a change! You were consistently spinning under the hands of God for a long time, and now you're immobile, sitting on the shelf to dry for twenty-four hours. But it seems like forever.

> "I've been sitting on the shelf for a long time. When is my ministry going to begin? When are others going to notice God's call on my life? Is God really going to use me to turn the world upside down for Him? Did God forget about me?"

On the drying shelf, Satan plants an expectation in your heart that God will fail you. He'll use the time that has passed and the weariness caused by waiting to demoralize you. And while you're languishing on the shelf wondering where God is, Satan will point to how God is acting to meet the needs of others to paint a vivid picture in your mind that God has not kept His promise to you.

All of Satan's strategies are designed to destroy your faith and cause you to question the goodness of God. The enemy knows that if he can get you to doubt God's goodness, you'll drop your shield of faith. The answer to his attempts to extinguish your faith is to fight discouragement and disappointment like the plague.

When we find ourselves on the drying shelf, we need to pray, "Lord, I'll stay in the wilderness my whole life if I must. I've found you in the desert, and you're all I need."

On the drying shelf you determine to never again doubt the goodness of God.

EMBRACING THE REFINER'S FIRE

The Lord then moves you from the shelf to the kiln—from the wilderness to the fire. You feel the relentless blaze. You begin to perspire. In the heat your heart is exposed. As the fire gets hotter the pain increases.

Fire's work is different from that of water. Water adds moisture, but fire transforms. It melts. It changes the whole structure. In the intense heat, things you thought you had already dealt with come to the surface.

You die to self. *Self* burns away. It evaporates in the fire.

You let go of your reputation, your fears, and your need to maintain control. You release idols, sin, compromise—anything that interferes with God's plan for your life. And you experience the pain of persecution like you never have before. God is enabling you to stand in any kind of ministry adversity.

In the kiln, you realize that the more you fear man, the less you fear God. You finally understand that it's not the reputation and approval of man that you need, it's being so deeply rooted in God that no matter the storms of life, you won't be moved. Once and for all, you let go of the fear of man and fully embrace the fear of the Lord.

There are impurities within each clay vessel that only the fire can purge. But also, in the fire is where you find God's power, passion, and presence.

In the kiln there's God's love, healing, and strength that you need to fulfill God's call on your life. Your heart softens. Insecurities melt away. You are rooted and grounded in the love of Christ. God has fashioned you with grace to endure. And you have within you a lingering fire for soul winning.

LEARNING TO PAY THE PRICE

Finally, the fire of the kiln is turned off. The kiln doors open. God removes you, and He places you in the glazing room. You're relieved to be out of the fire!

In the glazing room you sit on a table. And God begins to put the finishing touches on your ministry vessel. He lovingly brushes you with glaze and then carries you back to the kiln for . . . *the second firing*.

But this time you don't want to escape the kiln. You are willing to pay any price. You want the Refiner to do whatever needs to be done.

Now you understand there is a cost when it comes to maintaining your hunger for God, your intimacy with Jesus, and your spiritual power and authority. The calling you've had since you were in your mother's womb was birthed in the desert of loneliness, the crucible of rejection and opposition, and the weight of being set part. But you now recognize that it's only in the Refiner's Fire where you forsake everything for Christ, prepare to die for Him if required, and prepare to live for Him as His new creation.

There is an incredible price to pay to carry a powerful anointing. It's the Lord's desire for all to be chosen vessels, but few are willing to pay the price. You're pursuing the high calling and destiny the Lord has purposed for your life, therefore you'll never shrink back and are willing to pay any price.

It's during this second firing when your beautiful colors begin to appear; the fruit of the Spirit is evident in your life. The richness and depth of color are the result of your obedience to the Lord when times were tough, when you didn't understand, and when you didn't feel like obeying, but you obeyed anyway.

And when the Lord sees His reflection in you, He turns off the kiln.

GOD'S APPOINTED TIME

One of the greatest needs ministers have in the season of preparation is to receive the revelation of God's perfect timing. There are two words in the Greek for the word *time*:

> *chronos*—chronological time (seconds, minutes, hours, weeks, etc.), and,
>
> *kairos*—God's perfect, appointed time.

The enemy would keep us wrapped up in matters that pertain only to chronos time, counting the seconds. Chronos time causes stress. But when we walk in kairos time, we understand God's timing is perfect, and we patiently wait for it.

One of the major keys in operating in God's appointed time is to abide in Him. To abide means to remain or stay. Jesus is your source of life; cling to Him. If we abide in Him we will be in the right place, at the right time, doing the right thing.

As you abide in Jesus with simple childlike faith, you'll be graced with the patience needed to wait. *"If it seems slow in coming, wait patiently, for it will surely take place"* (Habakkuk 2:3b).

FOR IT WILL SURELY TAKE PLACE.
FOR IT WILL SURELY TAKE PLACE.
FOR IT WILL SURELY TAKE PLACE.

Due season always comes to those who remain faithful, those who are unwavering and uncompromising, and those who won't give up under pressure. If what you're waiting on hasn't happened yet, that doesn't mean it's not going to happen. With God it's not *IF* it's going to happen but *WHEN* it's going to happen. If God said it, He will do it. God has promised to use you in mighty ways. And that's all you need to know right now.

Talk to Abraham and Sarah about waiting. For twenty-five years they waited for the birth of Isaac (Genesis 12:1-4; 21:1-5). They waited, and waited, and waited. They wondered. And they wavered when they attempted to find a way on their own to fulfill God's promise. But when in their old age they held their son Isaac in their arms, they beheld God's faithfulness and His perfect *kairos* timing.

The realization of your calling *will* come to pass.

THE DISPLAY SHELF

At God's perfect, appointed time, He will place you on the display shelf in the spot He reserved for you since the foundation of the world. You are a vessel of honor. The display shelf represents ministry. If you aren't on that shelf yet, you will be as you faithfully cooperate with God's fashioning.

God wants to show you off. You've become His living epistle. People will look at you and see a vessel that was pliable and willing to be molded by God—someone who lives a fully surrendered life in Christ. And it's there, on the display shelf of ministry, where you point everyone to Jesus.

Your vessel is incredibly beautiful. You are full of the glory of the Lord and your transparent, gleaming glaze will reflect the splendor of Jesus. The steps in your journey to become God's honored vessel are sometimes painful. But that is necessary for transforming a lump of clay into an anointed vessel that reflects the glory of God. In time your pain will turn to joy.

Oh, sister, allow the Potter to conform you to the image of Christ. In this season of preparation, give Him permission to do whatever work in you that needs to be done. Ask God to put you in the Refiner's Fire. Embrace the fire of God so your heart will be on fire and you'll be able to impart that fire to others.

GIVING YOUR LUNCH TO JESUS

So what do you do while you're in the season of preparation? Be faithful with what God has already placed in your hands—like the little boy with the lunch.

When Jesus fed the 5,000 (John 6:5-13) He used the lunch of a little boy to work that miracle—five small loaves of bread and two fish. The child gave to Jesus what he had in his hands. Jesus took it, blessed it, broke it, multiplied it, and distributed it to the masses, with basketsful left over.

Friend, take a good look at your life. What has God given you to do right now? Work at it with all your might as an offering to God.

For example, are you waiting for an invitation to preach in front of an audience of thousands? While you wait for that platform, why don't you develop an online ministry on social media and teach whatever you would have taught if invited to speak at a large conference?

Are you called to pastor a church? Give yourself to the ministries of the church you are presently in. Are you called to be an itinerant evangelist? Begin winning souls in your city. Are you called to lead a Bible study? Invite a friend over for coffee and study the Bible together.

Instead of stewarding what God has already placed in their hands, some women wait for God to open a door while they sit idle. It simply doesn't work that way.

Prayer is a spiritual discipline you should also practice while you are in the season of preparation. What if you went on the offense and prayed for your future ministry in the waiting room of God's promises? Your intercession will pave the way for how God is going to move in your life. Prayer increases our capacity to receive more of Him.

These are the types of prayers that I prayed while waiting for my ministry to begin:

- Show me my purpose in life.
- Anoint me for what I am called to do.
- Give me wisdom and discernment.
- Root out all selfishness and pride from my life.
- Give me workers, givers, and intercessors for my future ministry.
- Give me a vast harvest of souls.
- Open doors for my ministry.
- Expose what needs to be exposed and reveal what needs to be revealed.
- Give me the gifts of the Holy Spirit needed for the ministry to which you've called me.
- Increase my pain threshold.

Unquestionably, Christians seldom utter the prayer "increase my pain threshold," but it remains crucial to the fulfillment of the callings God places on our lives. Christians will grow and mature only to the level of their pain threshold. If they draw a line in the sand and say, "No more pain!" they will stymie their seasons of preparation. (We'll talk more about this later.)

ACQUIRING THE FIRE

However, the most important thing you should do while you are waiting to be launched into your calling is to get filled (or stay filled) with the power of the Holy Spirit.

On the Day of Pentecost (Acts 2) 120 believers in the Upper Room were saturated with God. The fire that descended wasn't just a little candlewick upon their heads. It was the power of God that burned within them to win the world for Jesus Christ.

The essence of true Scriptural Christianity is doing the works of Jesus empowered by the fire of the Holy Spirit. The fire of God provides the indispensable power needed for effective witnessing. The book of Acts provides us with the plumb line for Spirit-empowered Christian living. Christians who are filled with the fire of the Holy Spirit are walking revivals.

Fire is identifiable. It's difficult to conceal. You don't have to advertise a natural fire. When there is a house fire, the local news channel just shows up. People come out of nowhere to watch it burn. They'll even stare at the aftermath of a fire—the ash and shell of the building. The fire of God, of course, is supernatural, and it's even more recognizable.

When you are consumed with the fire of the Holy Spirit, people will look at you and see the priorities of God, the activity of God, the power of God, and the love of God. They'll see Jesus in you.

The Holy Spirit moved with intense might on the day of Pentecost following the resurrection of Christ. And the Spirit still does today. Through the mighty Holy Spirit, God is active. He lives. And He speaks. The Holy Spirit enables natural humans to do supernatural exploits in order to fulfill the Great Commission.

I had an upper room experience that changed my life forever.

I had been frequenting a Christian bookstore in my local town. Each time I shopped in the store, I would strike up a conversation with the owner. Almost every time, she would talk to me about the fire of God. Honestly, I didn't pay much attention to what she was telling me, but she was relentless. She encouraged me to read the book of Acts with fresh eyes.

One particular day, after yet another conversation with the bookstore's proprietor, I went home and began reading Acts. When I got to the second chapter of Acts, a desperation for *MORE* of God came over me, and I fell to my knees praying, "Lord, I want everything you have for me!"

I stood on my feet and worshiped God. As I did, a light and heat, like I had never before experienced, flooded that upstairs bedroom of our small Cape Cod-style house. It was like someone turned on a stadium lamp that shone through my bedroom window. With tears streaming down my face, all I could do was proclaim my love for Jesus.

From that moment, my Christian walk has never been the same. That encounter with God changed my life forever. It felt like my spiritual engine was operating on all eight cylinders instead of just two. After that encounter, I prayed with fire, praised with fire, and won souls with fire. I was revived! And I burned for Jesus.

The impact that the fire of the Holy Spirit had on my life was immeasurable. Boy, was that Christian bookstore owner right! I needed the fire of God! And we all do.

It's the responsibility of every child of God to get on fire for God. But you've got to want it. You can't embrace entertainment over fire, comfort over fire, dullness over fire, status quo over fire, man's opinion over fire, or anything else over fire.

Paul wrote of over 500 people who saw Jesus after His death and resurrection (1 Corinthians 15:4-7). But there were far fewer mentioned as being there on the day of Pentecost when the fire fell. Don't be like the 380 who witnessed Jesus' resurrection but didn't show up to the Upper Room to wait for the gift the Father promised as Jesus had instructed (Acts 1:4). Instead, imitate the 120 who obeyed Jesus and waited in the Upper Room for the fire of God to fall on them.

But there's another attribute of fire, and it's one you need to understand. Fire can go out. Just because you were on fire for God at one time doesn't mean you are on fire for God now. If that's you, cry out to God for His fresh fire!

Honestly, there is no time to waste. There is an urgency in this hour.

These are the Last Days. We've got to stay sharp. We've got to stay keen. We've got to stay boiling hot for God. The salvation of souls depends on it. And the ability to continue to hear direction from God, moment-by-moment in these turbulent times, depends on it.

You may feel like a racehorse waiting for the gate to lift and hear the words, "And she's off!" But please don't start your ministry until you are baptized in the Holy Spirit. Jesus instructed the disciples to wait until they were filled with *"power from heaven"* (Luke 24:49). He is asking you to do the same.

The fire of God is still available today. It's the same fire the early Christians experienced in Jerusalem on the day of Pentecost. It's the same fire that filled me in the upstairs bedroom of my house in New Jersey thirty years ago. It isn't another fire. It's that same fire.

Ask the Holy Spirit to fill you with His fire. He will. He's been waiting for you to ask Him.

A PRAYER TO RECEIVE THE BAPTISM IN THE HOLY SPIRIT

Lord, I need your fire. I want to burn for you. All Consuming Fire, let your fire fall upon me. I ask you to fill me to overflowing. Saturate me with the fire of the Holy Spirit. I want to be on fire for you in every area of my life. Keep your fire burning inside me. Convict me if I'm ever tempted to let your fire go out. I receive your fire now by faith. From this day forward, I'm empowered to be your witness. I'll set the world ablaze with the gospel of Jesus Christ everywhere I go. I love you, Lord! In Jesus' name I pray. Amen.

CHAPTER 4

Satan's Plan of Sabotage

WHEN I WAS a brand-new, bright-eyed, bushy-tailed, and wet-behind-the-ears pastor, I knew with my help, all of the people in my church would walk in God's calling on their lives, because,

- Jesus is limitless God.
- Every person left to his or her own devices is limited.
- All limitations are now off when Jesus becomes Lord of someone's life.

While I continue to believe these truths with my whole heart, unfortunately there were many who did not fully own them. Why? Some continued to believe the lies of the enemy regarding who they are, what God can accomplish through these truths, and how much He can use them in ministry—thus thwarting God's call on their lives.

The enemy's lies are effective with far too many people. His lies are central in his plans to destroy God's work. And I assure you **Satan has a plan to use his lies to sabotage your destiny**. Please remember, the only power the enemy has over us exists when we agree with his lies! Our minds truly are the battlefield.

> One of the greatest joys of ministry for me has been watching Christians answer God's call on their lives. The greatest sorrow has been when they don't.

After spending decades in ministry, I've witnessed countless numbers of Christians *almost* answer their callings, *almost* use their gifts and talents to build the kingdom, and *almost* fulfill their destinies. Watching that play out has truly been one of the heartbreaks of ministry. And for the person who falls into the enemy's trap, the pain and regret are unbearable.

I'm so tired of *ALMOST!* Hopefully you are too!

It's impossible to fully answer God's call on your life while embracing the lies of the enemy. Oh you may walk in a partial fulfillment while embracing Satan's lies, but you'll do so with a spiritual limp.

Every time God gives you a larger assignment, or asks you to go to your next level, you'll return to a limiting belief if you don't replace lies with Truth. Worse yet, when you minister to others, you can pass your own limitations on to them. Ministry is both taught and caught. How we respond to the issues of life teaches others how they should respond to them.

Or, tragically, you may not answer God's call on your life at all.

I've seen this pattern over and over again: A Christian who wants more than anything to do great exploits for God steps out in faith to fulfill his or her destiny but trips right before crossing the threshold of opportunity.

Why? Because of the grave clothes that person is wearing.

Lazarus was terribly ill. His sisters sent word to Jesus (in effect summoning Jesus to pray for him). In the interim—before Jesus arrived where they lived—Lazarus died. His sisters thought all hope was lost. But with Jesus there is always hope, and His timing is always perfect!

Lazarus had been dead for a few days when Jesus arrived on the scene.

> *Then Jesus shouted, "Lazarus, come out!" And the dead man came out, his hands and feet bound in grave clothes, his face wrapped in a headcloth. Jesus told the people around Him, "Unwrap him and let him go!"* (John 11:43-44)

Lazarus was bound by grave clothes, and grave clothes represent the life we lived before we were born again—including the lies we believed. We were bound!

The moment we receive salvation, we're brand-new creatures in Christ Jesus. Our spirits, which were once dead, are now alive. But our souls (minds, wills, and emotions) remain unchanged and in desperate need of an encounter with the Word of God. We remove our grave clothes by renewing our mind with Truth. We take off worldly thinking and put on Word-of-God thinking.

> *Don't copy the behavior and customs of this world, but let God transform you into a new person by changing the way you think. Then you will learn to know God's will for you, which is good and pleasing and perfect.* (Romans 12:2)

Grave clothes often reveal and expose,

- Lies embraced.
- Truth to apply.
- Wisdom to employ.

- Spiritual disciplines to incorporate.
- Destructive habits to surrender.
- Sins from which to repent.
- Strongholds to break.
- Pain to heal.
- Priorities to be adjusted.
- Growth to transpire.

The *only* antidote for the lies of the enemy is the Truth of God's Word. So while there are probably multiple areas of our lives from which grave clothes need to be removed, we start every process by replacing lies with Truth. And then as we step out into ministry, we choose to believe what God has spoken instead of the lies Satan tells us. If the enemy's lies are left to stay, they become part of our belief system, and they'll put a limit on how much God can use us to change the world for Jesus Christ!

Sister, *you* are the only one who can stop the fulfillment of your calling! It's not your spouse, your pastor, your church, your denomination, or even the devil who can thwart God's plan. It's *YOU*, through self-limiting beliefs.

Satan hates it when believers are about to step into their destinies. He will use anything to try to stop it—fear, condemnation, insecurity, temptation, doubt, sin, desire for comfort, and so on.

Here is the typical scenario:

God opens a door of ministry in a believer's life.

As the believer's foot is about to cross the ministry threshold, right on cue, the enemy attacks with lies.

The believer succumbs to the attack by believing the lies of the enemy.

Satan's plan of sabotage is successful—the door is blocked, and the believer's calling is successfully thwarted!

It's no surprise that the enemy will try to steal a believer's destiny; it's guaranteed. It's part of Satan's job description (John 10:10). The real surprise for me, however, is how many believers fall prey to his plan.

To assist you in identifying possible areas of agreement with the lies of enemy, here are eight of the most common excuses that I've heard women called to ministry make for why they're not answering God's call.

1. I'm not enough.

Other versions of this are "I feel so unworthy," or "I don't have what it takes." This is the enemy diminishing you using feelings of unworthiness or insecurity. He does this to try to steal your voice, your identity, your authority, and ultimately your calling.

You're in good company. We see this same pattern in Scripture—when God raised up leaders in the Bible. First, God tells people what He wants to accomplish through them. Then unworthiness or insecurity attacks them because their callings are much bigger than they are. (By the way, your calling will *always* be bigger than you.) And then they make excuses for why they can't answer God's call.

- Moses: *"O Lord, I'm not very good with words . . .. I get tongue-tied, and my words get tangled"* (Exodus 4:10).
- Gideon: *"But Lord, how can I rescue Israel? My clan is the weakest in the whole tribe of Manasseh, and I am the least in my entire family!"* (Judges 6:15).
- Jeremiah: *"O Sovereign Lord, I can't speak for you! I'm too young!"* (Jeremiah 1:6).

Satan will even talk to you in the first person. "I'm a terrible person." "I'm not good enough." "Who would want to hear what I have to say?" If the enemy can deceive you into believing his lies through feelings of unworthiness or insecurity, he will have successfully reduced you, made you feel smaller, or less than adequate compared to others.

The answer is to focus on who *God* is in you! Residing in your spirit is the same power that raised Jesus from the dead, the nine fruits of the Holy Spirit, the nine gifts of the Holy Spirit, the glorious names of God, and His attributes. Also indwelling you is the glory of God, the God of breakthrough, the God of love, the Father of lights, the glorious unlimited resources of God, everything that pertains to life and godliness, and the holy of holies. In a unique way, you are the Ark of the Covenant with arms and legs.

Here is God's response to the excuse of "I'm not enough:"

Take your eyes off yourself and fix your gaze on Jesus.

2. **If you only knew me.**

This excuse is rooted either in condemnation or shame. When the enemy attacks with condemnation, he hammers you over the head with your past mistakes, sins, flops, failures . . . anything. (We all have them.) And then he places the hammer in your hand for you to do the same. We all have a past. You do. I do. The Apostle Paul did. And so has everyone who has ever lived (except for Jesus, who is perfect and without sin).

When you're battling shame, you feel flawed or defective. Guilt says, "I *made* a mistake," but shame says, "I *am* a mistake." Shame scrutinizes everything you've done wrong. It acts like a voice in your head that says you should've done this or you ought to have done that. Shame will tell you that you won't fit in and that you're damaged, inadequate, unlovable, deficient, weak, helpless, incompetent, or inferior.

Shame is internalized disgrace, humiliation, and degradation. It scrutinizes everything you've done wrong. It causes you to relate everything to yourself. Shame will cause you to turn any type of criticism of what you *do* into judgment of who you *are*. It can cause you to become defensive, sensitive, and argumentative in order to exonerate yourself. And if not, it will force you to admit your own inadequacies.

Even your walk with God can be affected by shame. It can shackle you to your past and erect a spiritual partition between you and God. You never feel good enough to approach God in prayer, because you can't put your past behind you.

Shame is one of the most devastating emotions there is. It acts as a corrosive agent to try to strip away who God has made you to be, thus stealing His call on your life. And when you hold onto shame it becomes your identity and acts as a demonic security blanket. This is why your identity must be solidly in Christ.

And here is God's response to this excuse:

Take your eyes off yourself and fix your gaze on Jesus.

3. **It will require me getting out of my comfort zone.**

We all love the comfort zone! Why? Flesh loves comfort. It hates to be challenged, stretched, and exposed to unfamiliar things and territory.

Satan will lie to you and tell you that life is good on Comfort Road. He'll point to other Christians who live there as well. The enemy will whisper sweet nothings in your ear. "Enjoy your life. Live your best life now. You deserve to be happy." However, comfort-zone Christianity equals death. Stay in your comfort zone and your dreams, gifts, and destiny will die a slow, painful death.

The opposite of comfort-zone Christianity is that experience described in Jesus' words to the crowd who followed Him. *"If any of you want to be my follower, you must give up your own way, take up your cross daily, and follow me"* (Luke 9:23).

UGH! Give up my own way? Take up my cross? But they aren't comfortable activities! Here's the thing. The opposite of the Kingdom of God is the kingdom of *ME*. When our will opposes God's will, we have a decision to make. Either follow Jesus or ourselves—God versus self.

Living for Jesus involves discomfort. Preaching the gospel involves discomfort. Loving your enemies involves discomfort. And answering your calling involves discomfort.

So instead of resisting discomfort, yield to it. Decide to abide in the *zone of discomfort*. Step out of the boat. Walk by faith. And obey God. To follow Jesus means your flesh will suffer. So be it. Obey anyway.

God's response to this excuse:

Take your eyes off yourself and fix your gaze on Jesus.

4. **No one will want to receive ministry from me.**

Self-sabotage! You're rejecting yourself before anyone else has a chance to reject you. We've all experienced rejection at various points in our lives, but those who battle rejection the most are those with deep, open wounds and scars from not feeling loved.

All of us have a basic need to be loved, wanted, and accepted. Rejection happens when someone makes us feel otherwise. A root of rejection forms when seeds of rejection are deeply planted in our hearts. The more we believe the lie that we aren't loved, wanted, or accepted, the stronger the root of rejection becomes.

A rejection spirit is eradicated when we believe the Truth of God's Word. And the Word says we are loved, wanted, and accepted by God. The love of God is the cure for rejection. When you have a revelation of God's love, rejection has no power over you.

If you don't experience freedom from rejection, you can allow rejection to stop the call of God on your life. Ministry is full of opportunities to experience rejection. In the morning someone in your church or ministry texts you to say, "God used you to save my life. I can't live without you." And by nightfall the same person can send you a message that says, "I'm leaving the church. Please don't contact me ever again."

This scenario has actually happened to me. The point is, various forms of rejection can happen at every turn in the ministry. Therefore, if you're not delivered from feelings of rejection, it will devastate, paralyze, and deeply wound you.

If you battle a root of rejection, meditate on the love of God. Ask Him for a deeper revelation of His love. Approach the place of prayer knowing how much God loves you. Instead of letting a root of rejection grow within you, let your own roots grow down into God's love for you.

> *Then Christ will make his home in your hearts as you trust in him. Your roots will grow down into God's love and keep you strong. And may you have the power to understand, as all God's people should, how wide, how long, how high, and how deep his love is. May you experience the love of Christ, though it is too great to understand fully. Then you will be made complete with all the fullness of life and power that comes from God.*
>
> (Ephesians 3:17-19)

God's response to this excuse:

Take your eyes off yourself and fix your gaze on Jesus. (Are you seeing a pattern here?)

5. I'm waiting until everything is just right to start.

I hear this excuse a lot, especially in answer to, "Have you launched your ministry yet?" At the root of this is perfectionism and procrastination—both enemies to your calling. Perfectionism is idolatry because, in essence, you're putting yourself on the same level with Jesus, who is the only perfect one. Women called to ministry will brag that they are perfectionists. Sister, this is nothing to brag about but a sin to avoid.

When people operate in perfectionism, they rely on themselves to do the work of ministry, not on God. Embrace the fact that you can do nothing perfectly, but strive for excellence in all you do. Every Kingdom leader needs to operate in excellence. But there is a huge disparity between excellence and perfection.

Excellence says, "I serve an excellent God, therefore I'm going to bring my very best to the table. But I'll rely one hundred percent on God to do it, supernaturally, through me."

Perfection says, "I'm going to flawlessly complete the task and won't move forward until I do."

Perfectionism waits until everything is perfect and all circumstances are right before stepping out into ministry. This leads to procrastination. If things aren't done perfectly, procrastinators cursed by perfectionism won't do it at all. Or if they do work on a task, it will never seem quite finished. In addition, they will move painstakingly slow to get the job done "just right."

Woman of God, much of ministry is flying the plane while you're building it. If we spend our years building the perfect plane down to the minutest, insignificant, unimportant detail, we will lag far behind God's timing. If we wait until things are perfect, we will never do anything for the Lord.

This also applies to personal trials, attacks from the enemy, and financial fitness. So many women have the attitude of, "I'll wait until this is over before I launch my ministry," or, "When I have the money, then I'll start my ministry." Delayed obedience is disobedience. Trust me when I say, when one personal problem is over, there'll be another one right around the corner.

The day we became born again, we voluntarily enlisted in the Army of God. As soldiers in God's army, we go from battle to battle to battle. Regardless of whether our battles are small skirmishes or battles as severe as a world war, we will always be engaged in some type of spiritual battle with the enemy of our soul.

God's response to this excuse:

Take your eyes off yourself and fix your gaze on Jesus.

6. I don't know enough.

Wait, you mean ME?

I wouldn't know how to begin.

I'm not a teacher.

I wouldn't be able to answer all their questions.

It's the enemy who injects this lie into our minds. He wants us to think we don't know enough to win souls, lay hands on the sick, cast out demons—in other words to answer our callings. The wrong mindset of "I don't know enough" has managed to kill the God-given destinies of many.

While God sometimes requires us to receive further training and education (so that we rightly handle the Word of Truth), we will never know enough. I received my Doctor of Ministry degree from a top accredited university, and I still don't know enough. As a matter of fact, the more I know the more I realize how little I know. We answer our calling out of love and obedience for the Lord, not on how much knowledge we presently have.

When my son was born, I didn't know anything about babies. I was an only child and had never been around children. I wondered, "How can I possibly be a good mother?"

Discharge day arrived. My beautiful new baby and I were going home. The maternity nurse entered my room with clipboard and pen. She rattled off questions from her "new mom" discharge checklist.

"Do you know how to change his diaper? Feed him? Burp him? Give him a bath?" My mind was swirling. My answers were, "No. No. No. No." The nurse must have seen the overwhelmed look on my face. And I think I tipped her off as to how clueless I was by asking if I had to set an alarm for feeding time, to which she answered, "Your baby is the alarm clock!"

The nurse gently set down her clipboard and calmed concerns, "I can tell you love your baby. The most important thing to remember is that babies need love, and I can already tell you have that down. Everything else will come to you."

She was absolutely right. I loved him more than anything in the world, and love took care of everything else.

Our love for Christ and His people fuels the engine of ministry. It's because of love that we pour our time, the Word, prayer, fellowship, wisdom, encouragement, and correction into the lives of God's people. Love takes care of the *I don't know enough.*

We also answer our callings out of obedience. Simply put, Jesus tells us to do it . . . so we do. Obedience is the lifestyle of a disciple. We obey God instantly even when it doesn't make sense, even if it hurts, or even if we don't know enough. We obey Him even when we don't see the benefit, when we don't feel qualified, or when it's inconvenient. We obey God completely and totally regardless of how much or how little we know. Partial obedience is disobedience.

When I became a Christian at twenty-six years old, I had zero knowledge of the Scriptures. I was a clean slate (no exaggeration). I didn't even know the basic children's Bible stories of Adam and Eve, and Noah and the ark. (I thought David and Goliath was a story about a boy and his dog!)

I endeavored to share with others whatever I learned. If my pastor preached on John 3:16, I found someone to whom I could explain John 3:16. When I learned the basics of prayer, I invited several friends over to my home for a prayer meeting to impart what little I knew about prayer. And I've never stopped doing this—ever learning and ever passing on what I've learned.

While we always want to grow in our knowledge of the Word (there is a big difference between a butcher and a neurosurgeon), don't let "I don't know enough" stop you from answering your calling.

> *The Holy Spirit will give you the words to say at the moment you need them.* (Luke 12:12)[2]

God's response to this excuse:
Take your eyes off yourself and fix your gaze on Jesus.

7. It's too hard being a woman in ministry.

First . . . *too hard?* Are you a follower of Christ? Is there anything you won't do for Jesus? As believers in Christ, we are called to have Galatians 2:20 lives: *"My old self has been crucified with Christ. It is no longer I who live, but Christ lives in me."*

The opposition that women in ministry face for being a *woman* in ministry is a form of persecution. I've encountered many women who were initially excited to pursue God's call until the hostility, antagonism, and resistance began—and it will. This especially happens when the criticism comes from family or those close to us.

They couldn't take the heat, so they got out of the kitchen. They weren't willing to endure persecution for Jesus' sake—a victory for the kingdom of darkness for sure. It's crucial to understand that experiencing persecution is a normal part of the Christian walk.

> *Yes, and everyone who wants to live a godly life in Christ Jesus will suffer persecution.* (2 Timothy 3:12)

> *Do you remember what I told you? "A slave is not greater than the master." Since they persecuted me, naturally they will persecute you. And if they had listened to me, they would listen to you.* (John 15:20)

> *God blesses those who are persecuted for doing right, for the Kingdom of Heaven is theirs. God blesses you when people mock*

2 Scripture taken from The Voice™. Copyright © 2012 by Ecclesia Bible Society. Used by permission. All rights reserved.

> *you and persecute you and lie about you and say all sorts of evil things against you because you are my followers. Be happy about it! Be very glad! For a great reward awaits you in heaven. And remember, the ancient prophets were persecuted in the same way.* (Matthew 5:10-12)

Second, this excuse clearly stems from a victim mentality. A victim mentality occurs when we see ourselves as the victim and not the victor. Classic victim mentality says, "Women in ministry get attacked more severely than our male counterparts."

Women in ministry don't have it harder than men in ministry. The persecution we receive is often simply different. Men receive attacks from the enemy that we don't, and vice versa. The devil is the devil no matter your gender. He is an equal opportunity enemy.

Push through any amount of persecution you receive for answering your calling. Accompanying God's call is the grace to endure opposition and any other fiery dart of the enemy. Give the enemy a black eye by giving God your *"YES!"*

God's response to this excuse:

Take your eyes off yourself and fix your gaze on Jesus.

8. I don't have as much to offer as other women.

This excuse comes from the voice of doubt and disbelief that God handpicked you for the ministry. You doubt God's sovereignty. You doubt His wisdom. You doubt He knows better than you. You doubt His plan. You doubt God!

"Someone else could do the work of ministry so much better," you mutter to yourself.

The world calls this *Imposter Syndrome*. It's when you feel like a fake or fraud. But it's nothing but doubt and unbelief.

Often when you first step into ministry it feels like when you were a little girl playing dress-up. Remember what it was like to put your tiny feet into your mother's high-heeled shoes that were many sizes too big? Instead of walking in them, you did a lot of sloshing around and many times fell. We have to grow into God's call on our lives.

God knows exactly what He's doing. He's God. He knows the beginning from the end. He knows your heart. He knows what He can accomplish through you. He knows what he placed you on this earth to do. He made you for a specific purpose. He has seen the entirety of your life and has still chosen *you*. And He doesn't make mistakes.

The longer we're in relationship with God, the greater measure of faith we should walk in. The more we know Him, the higher our level of trust should be. We should exhibit extraordinary faith in our extraordinary God. But why don't we walk by faith, especially when it comes to seeing ourselves through God's eyes?

Here lies the answer:

The opposite of walking by faith is walking by sight. It's when we walk by sight when doubt and unbelief creep in. When we keep our eyes on ourselves, we doubt God's judgment regarding us being ministry worthy.

The New Living Translation of the Bible says it this way, *"For we live by believing and not by seeing"* (2 Corinthians 5:7). Women called by God walk in extraordinary faith by keeping their eyes on Jesus, not on themselves. Their confident trust rests solely in Jesus. They keep their eyes on Him and His Word no matter their weaknesses, idiosyncrasies, and past failures (and we all have them). This, sister, is the good fight of faith—keeping our eyes on Jesus.

And as we keep our eyes on God, we intentionally magnify His enormity over ourselves. God is B-I-G. He is bigger than our abilities. Nothing is impossible with Him. One touch from God's hand will untangle the tightest, most complicated knot of our lives.

Do you know how big God's hand is? Isaiah provided the

answer. *"Who else has held the oceans in his hand? Who has measured off the heavens with his fingers?"* (Isaiah 40:12a). The span of God's hand (your hand's span is from the tip of your pinky finger to the tip of your thumb) measures the waters of the earth. God literally measures the Atlantic, Pacific, Indian, and Arctic Oceans with just His hand!

If that's how big God's hand is, can you imagine how *huge* He must be? As we magnify the enormity of God over our lives, we'll have no problem believing He will do all He has promised to do through us. Extraordinary faith expects God to do the extraordinary—even through me.

Often in the darkest of dark times, God divinely raises up His chosen instruments who will believe Him when others are falling away. Woman of God, we are living in that day. I want to be counted among those who trusted God and not in my humanness. If there is a Hall of Faith in heaven, I don't want there to be an empty spot where my picture was supposed to hang. No, I want my portrait to be among the greats like those listed in Hebrews chapter eleven—the people who walked by extraordinary faith.

Friend, stand stalwart against doubt and unbelief. Walk by faith and not by sight. Stand militant against lies and deception. And answer God's call on your life.

God's response to this excuse:

And for the last time I say: Take your eyes off yourself and fix your gaze on Jesus!

SABOTAGE-PROOF YOUR DESTINY

Now, here are seven steps to foiling Satan's plan to steal your destiny.

1. Don't be caught unaware and think the enemy will leave you alone.

   He won't. Expect it.

2. Think what you are thinking about.

   The enemy will inject lies into your mind about why you can't run through the door of opportunity. Therefore, you must examine your thoughts. Cast down the enemy's lies and speak God's Word. Pick up your weapons and fight!

3. Intentionally renew your mind with Scriptures that speak of your identity in Christ.

   When I was a young believer, I purchased a spiral bound index card notebook, wrote Scripture verses on their own separate cards, and read them out loud three times a day. On the days I battled lies from the enemy regarding my calling, I increased the readings to five times a day. In other words, do whatever it takes to combat the lies of the enemy.

4. What you behold, you become. Behold Jesus.

   Just like you'll never lose weight by staring at a box of donuts, you'll never walk in the fullness of your calling by gazing at yourself. Fix your eyes on Jesus and leave them there. Jesus wants to do the work of ministry through you, but if you keep your eyes on yourself, you'll lose sight of that and make it all about you.

5. Determine to step through the door of opportunity with confidence in the Lord.

   Get alone with the Lord, empty yourself of pride, fear, doubt, condemnation, sin, and so on, and ask God to fill you to overflowing with His Spirit.

6. Make an appointment with your pastor. Share your heart regarding stumbling blocks to your calling, and follow his or her wise counsel.

   God wants to remove your grave clothes, and sometimes He

does it with the assistance of the body of Christ (like he did with Lazarus). Sometimes extended counseling is needed. Other times deliverance is recommended to identify how the enemy got a toe hold and to permanently shut the doors you have opened. And still other times, all it takes is one conversation with your pastor.

7. *RUN* through the door God has opened for you!

   Don't tiptoe, stagger, or hold onto the doorpost for dear life. But *RUN* through with everything in you as if souls are depending on it. Because they are!

Woman of God, don't limp your way through your destiny. Open your heart before the Lord and pray something like this:

> Lord, I don't want anything to hinder me from stepping into my calling. Show me if I'm believing the lies of the enemy. Shine your Holy Spirit flashlight on any grave clothes still hanging off my life. Help me to line up my thoughts with your Word. Take the blinders off my eyes so I can see lies embraced, sin unrepented, Truth not applied, growth not allowed, wisdom not employed, wrong mindsets, and anything else that could sabotage my calling and thwart my relationship with you. I want to be completely and totally free to minister for you. From this point on, I won't let anything hinder your call on my life. Thank you for calling me to the ministry to set the world ablaze with the gospel of Jesus Christ. I love you, Lord! In Jesus' name I pray. Amen.

CHAPTER 5

Answering Critics, Objectors, and Naysayers

WOMAN OF GOD, from the moment you answer God's call until the day you graduate to heaven, critics will come against you and your ministry. This includes but is not limited to disapproving comments about your appearance, how you speak, what you say, the tone in which you say it, how you walk, what you eat, your family, your personality, your messages, the validity of God's call on your life, and on and on and on. (I've gotten them all.)

There are several reasons for this.

- You have an enemy who wants to paralyze you with fear, insecurity, doubt, and so forth, to stop your forward movement.
- You live a godly life in Christ Jesus. Therefore, you'll suffer persecution (2 Timothy 3:12). Destructive criticism is a form of persecution.

- You have a message that needs to be heard. If someone can discount the messenger, they can discount the message. The bottom line is that the enemy wants to stop the Word of the Lord being delivered through you.

Therefore, expect attacks to come through critics, objectors, and naysayers. Resign yourself to the fact that negative feedback is part and parcel of the ministry—no matter who you are or how long you've been in the ministry. As a matter of fact, ministers with large platforms will confirm that as their platform grew, so did critical attacks. New levels of ministry equal new devils. This is why it's important to keep your heart soft but have skin like Teflon so criticism doesn't stick.

It's important, however, to differentiate between criticism and godly correction. You'll confuse the two if you're not careful. Godly correction is sent by God. *"For the Lord disciplines those he loves"* (Hebrews 12:6a). And many times He will use those around us to do it. It's vital that we remain humble, teachable, and readily receive godly correction, because it's the pathway to becoming who God has called us to be.

> *Whoever heeds life-giving correction will be at home among the wise. Those who disregard discipline despise themselves, but the one who heeds correction gains understanding.*
>
> (Proverbs 15:31-32 NIV)

As a Kingdom leader, you'll receive both destructive criticism sent by the enemy as well as godly correction sent by God. Both are painful in the moment. The danger for you is in either taking everything to heart or taking nothing to heart.

There are ten questions to ask yourself to help you differentiate between ungodly criticism and godly correction.

1. Is it coming from someone God has placed in authority over me and who has permission to speak into my life?
2. Is it coming from someone who is known to have a critical spirit?
3. Is it coming from someone who is a known encourager and moves in the wisdom of God?
4. Is it coming from someone who has my absolute best interest at heart and wants to see me achieve God's potential for my life?
5. Is it coming from someone who has his or her own agenda?
6. Is it coming from someone who is spiritually mature and trying to help me see a blind spot? Or is it coming from someone immature in the Lord and who hasn't taken a plank out of his or her own eye before trying to take the speck out of mine? (Matthew 7:3).
7. Did it rob me of my identity in Christ or my purpose?
8. Does this person contribute to the vision of my ministry (uses his or her own gifts, invites people, sows financially, helps build my ministry, and so forth) or is he or she an armchair quarterback with no skin in the game?
9. Did I have peace in my spirit or a feeling of turmoil when the hurtful words were spoken? (In order to answer this question you'll have to separate out the pain.)
10. Did God send this person to speak these words to me? Or was he or she sent by the accuser of the brethren?

If you've determined the hurtful advice was destructive criticism, shake it off like you would a rattlesnake. Don't waste another moment thinking about what the person said. And when the enemy helps you recall the negative feedback, cast down negative imaginations and refuse to think on it. If it was sent in writing (snail mail, email, handed to you on a piece of paper) by all means don't save it. Toss it in the *Rubbermaid* file!

By the way, if you receive an anonymous letter (an unfortunate rite of ministry passage), discard it as quickly as possible, pray for the author's hurting heart, and move on. If the person who wrote the letter didn't have the courage to sign his or her name, it doesn't warrant a moment of consideration. If you have an assistant who opens your ministry mail, instruct him or her to throw all anonymous letters in the trash right away and not inform you about it. This will save you the unnecessary sting of a cowardly, disgruntled person who felt it was his or her job to express how awful you or your ministry is.

But if the Lord reveals it was godly correction, take it to heart. Right in the middle of the pain, humble yourself, bring it to the throne of God, and ask Him to help you make the necessary adjustment. I want to encourage you to have a change of heart regarding godly correction. Don't shudder when you think about it, but desire it.

Give permission to those in authority over you to speak anything into your life whenever the Lord leads them to do it—even if painful. High-capacity Kingdom leaders who do great exploits for the Lord Jesus Christ covet godly correction. Godly correction causes them to resemble their Savior more and is another opportunity to die to self.

DEFENDING YOUR CALLING

Although the validity of God's call on your life will be attacked your entire life in every season, from every angle, around every corner, and by both men and women, Jesus is worth any amount of persecution or suffering that we must endure for the sake of His call.

It's a true honor to be a trailblazer, pioneer, and co-laborer with Christ. I am humbled He chose me. And I know you feel the same.

Woman of God, as we discuss defending your calling, my goal is to,

- Encourage your calling through God's Word.
- Inspire you to launch into greater realms of ministry as you gain confidence in your calling.
- Help you establish a biblical theology of women in ministry.
- Teach you when to defend your calling and when not to.
- Assist you in defending your calling.

But first, let's peek into the thought processes of the enemy regarding women in ministry.

The devil's goal is to stop the gospel from being preached. So he twists the meaning of Scriptures regarding women proclaiming the gospel. Then he influences churches to establish an official doctrine prohibiting women from preaching the gospel. (This is simply a doctrine of demons.)

Those who ascribe to such a doctrinal position place spiritual duct tape over the mouths of every woman in their churches. And with that, the enemy has successfully silenced two-thirds of every church who holds to this doctrine. (Women don't comprise fifty percent of the Church, but two-thirds.)

The reason the devil does this is,

- To stop people from getting saved.

  Salvation only comes through the preaching of the Gospel of Jesus Christ.

- To attack the character of Almighty God.

  God created both male and female *in His image*. When the enemy devalues either gender in any way, he attempts to devalue the character of God.

- To try to dilute the blood of Jesus.

  When the enemy defames the callings of women in ministry, he tries to dilute the power of the cross. Jesus' blood is truly the *shatterer* of glass ceilings!

- To try to silence the Holy Spirit.

  The church that silences women will be found to silence the Holy Spirit as well.

- To try to bring into question the inerrancy and infallibility of God's Word.

  When the enemy twists Scripture, it results in the contradiction of the Truth of God's Word. Scripture never contradicts Scripture. He wants every human on the face of this earth to doubt the authenticity of God's Word.

I knew there was a calling on my life the day I became born again—thirty-three years ago. But I was completely naïve to the fact that people would come out against my calling. Not having been raised in a Christian home, I didn't understand there were churches who didn't believe women could be called into the ministry. What an eye opener it was for me to come to that stark realization through the person I looked to for spiritual leadership—my pastor.

It was March 2002. I was attending my church's women's retreat in Ocean City, New Jersey. Our guest speaker moved mightily in the gift of prophecy. On the last night of the retreat, she called everyone forward who wanted prayer. Her words graciously afforded me a glimpse into my future ministry.

As she prayed for me, she bent down, anointed my shins with oil, and proclaimed,

> I see your legs like tree trunks. I have seen other people's feet firmly planted as I have prayed for them, but never the entire leg. You are solid, not fragile, not easily tripped or offended. God has given you leadership legs because you are called to leadership. And tree-trunk legs are to enable you to stand in His call.

She then inquired if I was a minister. I told her that I wasn't, and she proceeded to pour the entire bottle of anointing oil over my head. It dripped down my hair onto my face and eyes.

"God has called you to be a teacher of the Word," she continued, "but He has also called you to be a pastor. You have a pastor-teacher calling." She repeated that several times and then called me "Reverend Jamie."

I was elated! My calling to ministry had finally been confirmed! Now nothing could stand in my way—or so I thought.

I went home from the retreat encouraged and filled with hope. I also knew I wanted to submit the directional, prophetic word I had just received to my pastor. Pastors don't just pastor the people; they pastor their gifts. Therefore, the Monday after the retreat, I did just that.

"No, women are not called to be pastors," my pastor responded as we met in his office.

He proceeded to give me one example after another of female senior pastors who were hugely unsuccessful in the ministry and had fallen flat on their faces. I sat speechless holding back the flood of tears that wanted to cascade down my cheeks like roaring rapids.

"If women were supposed to be ministers," my pastor continued, "Jesus would have chosen at least one female among the twelve apostles. Women need to stay home, take care of their husbands and children, and manage their households. That's where women belong."

Looking back, I find it interesting how he arrived at that erroneous opinion. The church he pastored was planted by a female pastor. She mentored him, poured into him, encouraged him, and corrected him. She was his spiritual mother. After she passed away, he became senior pastor of the church. He even had a picture of her in the hallway of the church to memorialize her.

As the conversation with my pastor concluded, I thanked him for his time and walked out of the meeting as quickly as I could. Safely in my car, hot tears flowed down my face, stinging my cheeks. I had walked into the meeting exhilarated, but I walked out more devastated and disappointed than I had ever been in my entire life.

It's important to note that the church I attended didn't have a doctrinal statement prohibiting women in ministry. Neither did the denomination to which the church belonged. As a matter of fact, the denomination itself is inclusive to both genders regarding ministry credentials. Sometimes doctrine against women ministers is unwritten and unspoken but just as dangerous as if it had been written. My pastor obviously had a personal bias against women in ministry.

In the privacy of my car, with the windows rolled up, I cried out to God.

"Deliver me! Deliver me from this church! Your call on my life will never come to pass here! Deliver me!"

My loving, compassionate, gracious God wrapped His arms around me and whispered, "Trust me, trust me, trust me. The very person who you thought would obstruct your calling will be the very person I will use to launch you into full-time ministry. When I promote you, people will say, 'Only God could have done that!'"

In that moment I had a decision to make. Was I going to leave the church where I knew God planted me and try to make my calling come to pass somewhere else? (That was what my flesh was speaking.) Or would I stay in God's perfect will, believe the promise He had given, and trust Him? I decided the latter was what the Holy Spirit was leading me to do, and I determined to take God at His word.

The Lord is true to His word, and about four years later, my pastor, who had adamantly opposed my calling, was the one God used to launch me into the ministry! God is truly faithful!

Some women are waiting for a man to open the door to ministry. But a man already has. And His name is *Jesus*.

But since that first conversation with my pastor, many have opposed my calling to ministry including,

- Male ministers (both inside and outside my denomination).
- Pastor's wives. (For some reason they have been among my harshest critics.)
- Visitors to my church.
- People I've looked to for leadership.
- Hosts of Christian programs where I've been a guest (refusing to introduce me as *Pastor* Jamie Morgan).
- Internet trolls. (They spend their day trolling social media for women in ministry to bash.)
- Theology stalkers. (For fifteen years a man called my church answering machine several times a week to inform me I was going to hell for preaching the gospel.)
- People I considered friends.

So how do you know when to defend your calling to your critics or ignore them altogether? Knowing whether or not the critic genuinely wants to know what Scriptures teach about the subject will be the determining factor.

Sometimes your critics were raised in a Calvinistic church that prohibited women in ministry, and they're just parroting what they've been taught their entire lives. But if you sat down with them for a Bible study on the topic, they would change their thinking.

Still others want to argue—and argue and argue. You could invite the top theologians on the subject to do a deep study with them, and your critics would simply dig their heels further into the sand and continue to argue their points. If I discern this is the case, I say something like, "You sit here and argue, but I'm going to go out and win souls!"

I say it in a jovial manner, but I get my point across. In the end they know that neither they nor anyone else will not stop me from fulfilling my calling. Friend, you've got to make the decision that no amount of criticism will prevent you from advancing the Kingdom in your area of ministry specialization.

My life verse is found in Acts 28. *"He* [Paul] *proclaimed the kingdom of God and taught about the Lord Jesus Christ—with all boldness and without hindrance"* (Acts 28:31 NIV). God has given me tree trunk legs to enable me to stand in adversity—a special grace to continue building the Kingdom no matter who or what comes against me. And He has given that same grace to you as well!

DEVELOPING A PERSONAL THEOLOGY OF WOMEN IN MINISTRY

It's crucial that you formulate a theological defense for women in ministry. This will not only assist you in answering naysayers but also allow you to gain confidence to stand firm in your calling. How can you convince someone else of something if you're unsure about it yourself?

To help you get started with developing your theological defense, let's examine the most common argument used by those who oppose a woman's calling to ministry.

The two predominant Scriptures critics repeatedly hurl at us like stones to attack our callings are First Corinthians 14:33-35 and First Timothy 2:11-12. The two-passage view the critics promote, versus the whole counsel of God, prohibits countless women from pastoring churches, becoming board members, and preaching sermons. The incorrect, skewed interpretations of these two passages of Scripture have frustrated and diminished the gifts, talents, and mantles of many women called to biblical leadership.

Because of the mishandling of Scripture, the enemy has been able to silence the mouths of many women to prevent them from participating in the Great Commission. As critics use these two verses, they disregard the Old Testament examples of women like Huldah, Deborah, and Miriam. And the ministries of New Testament women such as Priscilla, Phoebe, and Junia remain largely overlooked.

The only antidote for these injustices resides in discovering Paul's original intent when he penned those words to both the Corinthian believers and Timothy. For starters, we will discover that he was dealing with "isolated issues that troubled those two specific congregations."[3]

Paul told the church in Corinth,

> *For God is not a God of disorder but of peace—as in all the congregations of the Lord's people. Women should remain silent in the churches. They are not allowed to speak, but must be in submission, as the law says. If they want to inquire about something, they should ask their own husbands at home; for it is disgraceful for a woman to speak in the church.*
>
> (1 Corinthians. 14:33-35 NIV)

In this passage, Paul addressed a specific group of women who

3 Gordon D. Fee and Douglas Stuart, *How to Read the Bible for All Its Worth* (Grand Rapids, MI:Zondervan, 2003), p. 28.

kept disrupting the service by asking inconsequential questions.[4] The universal application from this passage remains this: "Do not exercise your freedoms at the expense of others."[5] An example of a specific application might be, "Students who did not do their homework should not ask silly questions in class."[6]

Furthermore, in the same chapter of First Corinthians, the Apostle Paul instructed a group of people to either keep quiet or stop speaking in two other separate situations—when people are speaking in tongues (v.28), and when people are prophesying (v.30).[7]

It's apparent that "Paul's 'be silent' [admonition] was not an 'absolutely-forever-under-every-circumstance-and-at-all-times' injunction against those who spoke in tongues, prophesied or women."[8] Paul instructed the women that "we want you to learn, but not at the expense of others."[9]

Then, Paul instructed Timothy.

> *A woman should learn in quietness and full submission. I do not permit a woman to teach or to assume authority over a man; she must be quiet.* (1 Timothy 2:11-12 NIV).

In this passage, Paul was addressing a specific group of women who were presenting erroneous teaching.[10] The universal principle

---

4 Craig S. Keener, *Paul, Women and Wives* (Grand Rapids, MI: Baker Academic, 1992), p. 17.

5 Deborah M. Gill, "Biblical Theology of Women in Leadership" (class notes for Core 2 Course at Assemblies of God Theological Seminary, Springfield, MO, February 23, 2016).

6 Craig S. Keener, *Paul, Women and Wives* (Grand Rapids, MI: Baker Academic, 1992), p . 88.

7 Deborah M. Gill and Barbara Cavaness, *God's Women Then and Now* (Colorado Springs: Authentic Books, 2009), p. 127.

8 Loren Cunningham and David Joel Hamilton, *Why Not Women?* Seattle: Youth with a Mission Publishing, 2000, p. 96.

9 Deborah M. Gill, *Biblical Theology of Women in Leadership.*

10 Craig S. Keener, *Paul, Women and Wives* (Grand Rapids, MI: Baker Academic, 1992), p. 108.

in this passage is that "Paul didn't make women taboo; he made heresy taboo."[11] Today's application is that order needs to be kept in the Church for discipleship to take place.[12]

Revisiting the conversation I had with my pastor decades ago with the knowledge I have today, I would have handled it a lot differently. With honor and respect I would have defended the call of God on my life. As much as I loved my pastor, I should have stood firm in my calling.

If I had understood things then as I do now, I would have countered that Jesus *did*, in fact, choose twelve men. And they were all Jewish. So using my pastor's reasoning, if Jesus precluded women from ministry, then all *Gentile men* would have been excluded from ministry as well.[13] I would have continued by demonstrating from the Bible that both women and Gentile men held leadership positions in the early Church after the Twelve began their ministries. Therefore, women and Gentiles can also serve in biblical leadership roles today.[14]

Furthermore, I would have explained that Jesus was groundbreaking in His inclusiveness of women, both in rhetoric and treatment. Jesus reached out to, and cared for, both genders equally. He taught women, included them in doctrinal discourses and parables, and incorporated them into His larger group of disciples. Jesus did all of this in a cultural climate in which there was severe discrimination and mistreatment of women.[15] In those

11 Loren Cunningham and David Joel Hamilton, *Why Not Women?* Seattle: Youth with a Mission Publishing, 2000, p. 203.

12 Deborah M. Gill and Barbara Cavaness, *God's Women Then and Now* (Colorado Springs: Authentic Books, 2009), p. 158.

13 Deborah M. Gill, *Biblical Theology of Women in Leadership*.

14 Deborah M. Gill, *The Biblical Liberated Woman, Paraclete* 29 (1995): p. 9.

15 Deborah M. Gill and Barbara Cavaness, *God's Women Then and Now* (Colorado Springs: Authentic Books, 2009), pp. 73-82.

days, Jewish men didn't even publicly acknowledge women when entering a room.[16]

I would also have made the strong point that both genders have shared origins as well as common destinies. Both man and woman became inseparably connected during Creation, and both fell together when they disobeyed God in the Garden. Because of these two things, their destinies are also forever linked. They are both, in the same exact way, lost in sin and in need of the Redeemer.[17]

I would have followed by sharing with my pastor that the apostle Paul illustrated God's intentions for the life of the Church with these words to the Galatians:

> *There is neither Jew nor Gentile, neither slave nor free, nor is there male and female, for you are all one in Christ Jesus.*
> (Galatians 3:28 NIV)

I then would have read the list of women Paul cited in Romans chapter sixteen (Phoebe, Priscilla, Junia, Mary, etc.), who held leadership positions in the Early Church.

Lastly, I would have said that below the cross of Christ Jesus is the most level ground there is—where women and men stand on equal footing.

MINISTRY CONFESSIONS

I highly suggest that every woman called into the ministry craft her own ministry confession—a one-minute elevator speech that briefly articulates her calling. Review it often, every day if needed. I did exactly that. When I first started in the ministry I read it aloud to myself before every service and at any time when the enemy tried to tell me I wasn't called, or when discouragement tried to set in.

16 Deborah M. Gill, *Biblical Theology of Women in Leadership.*

17 Loren Cunningham and David Joel Hamilton, *Why Not Women?* Seattle: Youth with a Mission Publishing, 2000, p. 93.

Here is my ministry confession:

I am called by God to be a minister of the gospel.
He has anointed me, appointed me, and equipped me for
such a time as this to fulfill the Great Commission.

I stand firm in my calling.

I have been given a mandate from God to preach the
gospel, win the lost, lay hands on the sick, cast out demons,
and mentor women in ministry—all of which I do
with great boldness and without hindrance.

I stand firm in my calling.

My feet are beautiful, my words are full of power,
my mind is filled with wisdom, my eyes are fixed on Jesus,
and my hand is to the plow.

I stand firm in my calling.

I am a daughter of God, upon whom He
has poured His Spirit. God chooses whom
He chooses—and He has chosen me.

I stand firm in my calling.

Sister, I urge you to stand firm in your calling, too.

CHAPTER 6

Prayer: Your Ministry's Immune System

MY GOAL FOR this chapter is simple: That it will encourage you to be driven to your knees in prayer—and that you'll stay there.

Prayer precedes the launch of your ministry, undergirds your ministry, sustains your ministry, grows your ministry, and produces disciples who are driven to their knees in prayer because of your ministry. God has put all that He is, and all that He has, at the disposal of prayer. But more importantly, intimacy with Jesus is only found in the place of prayer.

Prayer, prayer, and more prayer
must be a core value of your ministry.

This cannot be overemphasized. If prayer is not a core value of your ministry, the effects of that will be evident. *"Unless the* L*ORD* *builds a house, the work of the builders is wasted"* (Psalm 127:1a). The Lord will build your ministry as you travail in prayer, as you obey what He tells you in prayer, and as you commit your work to prayer.

Prayer will also keep your fire for God red-hot. One believer whose heart has been set on fire in her prayer closet can ignite a million candles. All it takes is one flame. I want to be that flame of prayer. And sister, I'm fully convinced you do as well.

Prayer is the greatest, most eternally beneficial way you can invest your time in the work of ministry. It's so important that the Apostles in the book of Acts knew spending time in prayer and teaching the Word had to come before all other ministry duties (Acts 6:3-4). Prayer is the most Christlike activity in which you can engage.

Jesus constantly makes intercession for us before the Father (Hebrews 7:25). And oh how it pleases Him when we make intercession before the Father! Prayer is the greatest, most rewarding investment you can make while on this earth. And it's the most precious gift you can give to Jesus—and to yourself.

Also, your prayers will outlive you; they're eternal. They'll continue to have an effect and move the heart of God even after you're gone. All of this and more is why Satan wants to keep you off your knees. This is why he fights you so.

THE RESULTS OF PRAYERLESSNESS

Our human bodies' immune systems are marvelous creations of God. When they are strong and working properly, optimal health ensues. Disease is eradicated before one symptom appears. When we have a robust immune system our energy levels are high, and we're full of life.

But when someone's immune system is compromised, they're vulnerable to illness. They experience frequent infections and heal much slower. They can also feel weak, become fatigued, and experience weight loss. Immune deficiency can lead to loss of life.

Prayer is the immune system of the follower of Christ—and of your ministry.

Without a consistent prayer life, our relationship with God will be anemic and shallow. We'll become spiritually emaciated and lose our appetite for things of God. Without a vibrant prayer life, powerlessness will overtake our ministries and make us defenseless against the attacks of the enemy.

Prayerlessness is a killer disease to both our Christian walk and ministry. Ask any minister who has fallen from grace. They won't hesitate to tell you their decent into sin began when they spent less and less time with Jesus in prayer.

The fall of man brought prayerlessness. The moment sin entered, Adam and Eve hid from the Lord (Genesis 3:1-8). This is where prayerlessness was born—in the heart of man in the Garden of Eden. When Adam and Eve hid from God, they turned their backs on the presence of God, fellowship with God, and communion with God. Prayerlessness is *hiding*.

People are still hiding from God. When someone doesn't pray it's a result of the fall. When the flesh is in control there is little to no prayer life. Until we see God face to face, we commune with Him in prayer. The only avenue to continually see God, hear His voice, and touch Him in our ministries, is through the vehicle of prayer.

As a result of prayerlessness, we won't hear the Lord's voice. Therefore, we won't receive needed counsel, direction, wisdom, and guidance for our lives and ministries. It's as we seek the Lord in prayer when God gives us creative ideas and solutions. Without

Him, our ideas will be shallow and one-dimensional, and we'll be the ones guiding our own lives and ministries—*a scary proposition indeed.*

As a result of prayerlessness, we won't be everything God has called us to be—and neither will our ministries. A Christian will never rise above his or her prayer life. A church will never rise above the prayer lives of its members. And a ministry will never rise above the prayer life of the minister and the intercessors she has surrounded herself with (more on that later).

As a result of prayerlessness, we will become weak and can easily fall into temptation. This can lead ministers to getting drained, diminished, distressed, and depleted. We'll live our daily lives and do the work of ministry in our strength instead of the Lord's.

And when we're weak, we won't be able to resist the wiles of the enemy. Sins we never dreamed we would ever fall into, or areas of deception we never pictured we could succumb to, will emerge if we don't have daily fellowship with God.

We live in a world that is constantly pulling at us. Add to that the never-ending busyness of ministry. It's crucial that we remain spiritually strong to walk against the tide of this world and the attacks of the enemy. As Charles Spurgeon said, "Be careful when picking up sticks, your fire doesn't go out." It's only through prayer that our fire doesn't go out.

Prayer isn't the sideshow for the minister of the gospel, but the main event—like we see in the book of Acts.

ACTS—OUR PRAYER PATTERN

The book of Acts remains the blueprint for the Church and is a portrait of Christians in the throes of revival. It's interesting to note that the entire Bible records more than 650 prayers. However, the book of Acts contains more references to prayer than any other book. This demonstrates the strong correlation between prayer and the power and presence of God.

In the book of Acts,

- Prayer birthed the Church (Acts 2:1-4).
- The first Christians devoted themselves to prayer (Acts 2:42).
- They protected prayer from the busyness of their hurried schedule (Acts 6:1-4).
- They gave themselves constantly to prayer (Acts 1:14).
- Prayer was the environment in which the Holy Spirit poured himself out (Acts 2:1-4; 8:15; 10:9-13, 30).
- There are thirty references to prayer.
- There were fourteen corporate prayer meetings.
- Prayer was the breath of the early Church.
- Christians were walking revivals because of prayer.

If we desire an outpouring of the Holy Spirit in our ministries, we need to prioritize prayer in the same way. The connection between prayer and revival in the Book of Acts clearly establishes that prayer needs to be the focal point of our lives. Nothing else will generate the same results.

However, the primary motive of our prayers needs to be this:

We want more of Jesus.

Any prayer that comes from the motive of wanting more of Jesus is a biblical prayer for the fire to fall on our ministries. Any revival prayer that is self-driven with the intention of making up for our deficiencies or improving our lives isn't a biblical revival prayer.

Acts 4:23-31 illustrates the value those new Christians placed on prayer as well as the power of God that is generated from prayer.

After hearing that Peter and John were released from prison for preaching the gospel, the believers lifted their voices in prayer. This was the result:

> *After this prayer, the meeting place shook, and they were all filled with the Holy Spirit. Then they preached the word of God with boldness.* (Acts 4:31)

The Holy Spirit made His manifest presence seen and felt as the early believers gathered in prayer. After their room-shaking prayer, God filled them with His Spirit, enabling them to preach the Word of God with boldness. When we pray, God's power is released from heaven. Our prayers go up, and God's power comes down. Conversely, if our prayers don't go up, God's power doesn't come down.

God longs to bring His lukewarm, backslidden, spiritually asleep, and apathetic Church back to life. And He wants to use you to do it. Partner with Him in prayer, first for intimacy with Jesus, then for the rain of the Holy Spirit to soak your ministry. And live in expectation of the revival God so desperately wants to send!

THE ONE THING

Little did sisters Martha and Mary know they would go down in Bible history as the poster children of daily devotions. Martha was famous for letting distractions thwart her time with Jesus. (Oh God, please don't ever let me become famous for that.) And Mary was well known for her commitment to sitting at Jesus' feet.

Martha took great issue with Jesus for letting Mary just sit there before Him listening to Him speak while Martha prepared dinner. The more our lives are GO-GO-GO, the more self-important we become. Busyness and self-importance go hand-in-hand.

Jesus answered Martha's it's-not-fair complaint like this:

> *My dear Martha, you are worried and upset over all these*

details! There is only one thing worth being concerned about. Mary has discovered it, and it will not be taken away from her. (Luke 10:41-42)

Who changes the most when I pray? Me! How do I close the gap between who I am now and who God has called me to be? *Prayer!*

In that secret place, God comforts me, pours His liquid love upon me, and imparts to me His passion for souls. It's in the place of prayer where the Holy Spirit, in the fireplace of my heart, sets me on fire for Him. It's through prayer where I cultivate a hunger and thirst for God. It's in prayer when I receive life-giving oxygen to keep burning for Him. If my prayer time becomes erratic, my fire for God is dampened.

Your daily, divine appointment with God is the solitary most important event of your day.

When I come to God in prayer, I create a place where the Holy Spirit is welcome. God responds to asking, and prayer is the place I ask God to pour His Spirit upon my thirsty heart. Prayer also makes the difference between the rain of the Holy Spirit falling on either a heart of concrete or thirsty ground.

Prayer is my way of cooperating with God to create a big enough reservoir to contain an outpouring of God's Spirit. Prayer increases my capacity to receive more of Him. And as I cry out to Him, He breaks me, shapes me, and gets me to the point of deeper desperation and dependency on Him.

I go to my prayer nook to spend time with my Savior every morning—no matter how many ministry tasks I have ahead of me that day. With sunlight streaming through my windows and the occasional view of a blue jay perching on its feeder, I focus my attention on Jesus and draw near to Him. Curled up on my striped, overstuffed "prayer chair," I reach for my Bible, pen, and prayer journal and begin feasting on the living Word of God.

Then I talk to God using words that one would use with a dear friend of thirty-three years. I usually start like this: "Lord, I've come to meet with you. Share your heart with me."

I spend a few minutes in silence, giving God time and space to speak. Then I share my heart with Him. He talks to me. And I talk to Him. And He talks to me. And I talk to Him. And day-by-day, daily devotion after daily devotion, I'm cultivating an intensely personal, passionate relationship with Almighty God.

THE POWER OF PRAYING IN TONGUES

I also pray in tongues as I'm sitting at the feet of Jesus. And I pray in tongues much all throughout the day.

I'm not a fan of maraschino cherries, the kind of cherries used to top an ice cream sundae. I love everything about ice cream sundaes—the ice cream, butterscotch topping, whipped cream, walnuts, and sprinkles (I know, I'm making you hungry!)—all except for the cherry. The cherry ruins the sundae. For me, fruit and ice cream just don't mix!

I'm so adamant about my aversion for cherries (gee, can you tell?), that when I order an ice cream sundae at a restaurant, I tell the waiter, "Please leave off the cherry." And then just in case the waiter didn't hear me the first time, I say, "Please, no cherry." For me, the cherry is completely optional. It's just not essential to my ice-cream-sundae-eating experience.

Some people view praying in tongues like I do the cherry on a sundae—optional and non-essential to their relationships with God. But woman of God, if that is you, I implore you to reconsider. You won't be able to minister as effectively as you could without the power of praying in tongues.

Praying in tongues will help you pray God's perfect will for your life and ministry.

> *And the Holy Spirit helps us in our weakness. For example, we don't know what God wants us to pray for. But the Holy Spirit prays for us with groanings that cannot be expressed in words. And the Father who knows all hearts knows what the Spirit is saying, for the Spirit pleads for us believers in harmony with God's own will.* (Romans 8:26-27)

You're praying for a person or situation every conceivable way you know how, but you're still at a loss for words. Has that happened to you? It's happened to me too. That's because we don't know another person's heart; nor do we know all the factors involved in any given situation. But God does. When we pray in our personal prayer language—given to us by God—we connect directly with the Holy Spirit, bypass our intellect, and allow the Him to pray His perfect will through us.

Praying in tongues also helps us to pray the mysteries of God.

> *For if you have the ability to speak in tongues, you will be talking only to God, since people won't be able to understand you. You will be speaking by the power of the Spirit, but it will all be mysterious.* (1 Corinthians 14:2).

As you pray in the Spirit, you'll pray for people, places, and things on God's heart, even if they're not on your prayer list or anywhere on your radar. For example, when you spend time praying in tongues, you could be praying for,

- The government of the nation of Kenya.
- The sick in a hospital in Croatia.
- An unsaved person in Boise, Idaho.

- A persecuted Christian imprisoned in communist China.
- A future event in your own life for which you would have no knowledge.
- A spiritual warfare strategy to thwart a planned demonic attack against your ministry.

Praying in tongues helps to strengthen your Christian walk as well. *"A person who speaks in tongues is strengthened personally"* (1 Corinthians 14:4a). The word "strengthened" in this Scripture means to edify, to build up, or to recharge. Praying in your personal prayer language will help you walk in the Spirit and not in the flesh because you are spiritually strong.

Therefore, I want to encourage you to pray in tongues when,

- You don't feel very spiritual.
- You're being sorely tempted.
- You feel under pressure.
- You are battling depression or fear.
- You need victory in a particular area of your life.
- Your emotions are like a roller coaster.
- You can feel you're in the flesh and need to quickly shift to the Spirit.
- You need peace and rest in your soul.
- You have doubt, uncertainty, confusion, or frustration.

Sister, at the first sign of a spiritual emergency, *hit it with tongues!*

My challenge to you is this: Pray in tongues twenty minutes per day. That's not some legalistic or mystical number, only a good goal. And while you do, focus on Jesus on His throne or the Holy

Spirit on the inside of you (not your store list). The impact that praying in the Holy Spirit will make on your Christian walk and ministry is immeasurable.

The bottom line is, when you set time aside each day with the Lord, you experience *Him*. Developing a deep relationship with the *Pearl of Great Price*, the *Bright Morning Star*, and the *Lily of the Valley* is the reward. And it whets your appetite for more of Him. Time spent with God causes us to crave more of God.

INCORPORATE FASTING INTO YOUR PRAYER LIFE

As followers of Christ, we do what He does. When Jesus walked the earth, He fasted. That's really all we need to know. Jesus fasted; so we should fast. For the minister of the gospel, fasting should be purposeful and intentional.

Jesus gave fasting instructions in the Sermon on the Mount. When speaking of fasting He began, *"But when you fast . . ."* (Matthew 6:17). Notice He didn't say, "But *if* you fast. . . ." Comparatively, Jesus used the same words regarding giving and prayer. *"But when you give . . ."* (Matthew 6:3), and, *"But when you pray . . ."* (Matthew 6:6).

It's a given that Christians fast, just as it's assumed believers will also give and pray. Fasting is normal Christianity.

The twelve disciples were approached by the desperate father of a demon-possessed boy to pray for his son, but they couldn't cast the demons out of him. After Jesus ministered complete freedom to the boy, His disciples questioned why they weren't able to do it.

Jesus' response was, *". . . this kind does not go out except by prayer and fasting"* (Matthew 17:21 NKJV).

Fasting adds spiritual *D-Y-N-A-M-I-T-E* to our prayer lives.

The early Church was committed to fasting and prayer. Many who have studied Church history say that in the early days of the Church, Christians fasted an average of two days per week. Prayer, coupled with fasting, birthed and sustained the greatest move of God this world has ever seen. Yet, fasting remains the most undervalued, underemphasized, and underutilized spiritual treasure in today's Church.

I've conducted periodic fasts my entire Christian walk. Before I fast, I ask God what type and length of fast He would have me undertake. I've fasted one meal, two meals, a half day (fasting until 3:00 PM), 24 hours, three days, ten days, and the *Daniel fast* (eating only fruits, vegetables, and grains). I have Christian friends who have conducted 21 day and 40 day fasts. (Remember to consult your doctor before starting any type of fast. If you can't fast for medical reasons, fast and pray between meals.)

My reasons for fasting are many and varied, but include:

- For needed breakthrough
- To regain spiritual hunger
- To humble myself before God
- When making a major life decision
- When I'm struggling with submitting to God's will
- When I'm reverting back to religion from relationship
- To give teeth to repentance
- To get my cutting edge back in prayer
- When I'm feeling overwhelmed
- When embarking on a new year or ministry assignment

- To clearly hear God's voice
- To ready myself for the return of Christ
- For personal revival

Before I was in the ministry, I had Lyme Disease. It was a fiery trial that seemed to go on with no end in sight, lasting fifteen long years. I awoke every single morning to flu-like symptoms yet had an entire day's activities ahead. I was a full-time wife, mom, employee, and ministry worker. There were many days I couldn't put one foot in front of the other. However, I stood on God's promises and relied on His strength and grace to see me through.

One particular day, in agony and desperation I cried out to the Lord for help. I felt like I couldn't take it anymore. After I prayed, I felt impressed to go on a three day fast that I began the following morning. Although I don't exactly know when my healing manifested itself, at the end of the three days all of the Lyme Disease symptoms had disappeared.

Why did it take fifteen years for my healing to appear? Why did God choose to heal me during that particular three day fast when I had fasted many times during the course of that painful season? To this day, I still don't know the answers to these questions.

While I don't presume this is God's method for everyone battling chronic illness, my day of breakthrough came during that fast. We all have different relationships with God, and His plan for each one of us is perfect.

When we fast, we deny ourselves the pleasure of food to gain greater intimacy with God. We don't fast to garner God's favor. His favor is something we already possess. Fasting helps us to align with God's will, plans, and purposes. And it encourages us to hunger after God more fully. When we empty ourselves, God will fill us.

Some helpful fasting pointers:

- Biblical fasting is giving up food.

  Abstaining from TV or social media, while fantastic ideas that can be coupled with fasting, isn't fasting. Food is a basic need; TV and social media aren't.

- Spiritually prepare before your fast.

  Ask God to ready your heart. Repent from sin, pride, wrong attitudes, and unforgiveness. Keep a journal during your fast to write down your fasting goals and record your prayer and fasting adventures with God.

- Remember to pray and read God's Word.

  This may seem obvious, but fasting without prayer and meditating on the Word is . . . well . . . *dieting*. We fast to focus more completely on God. But be aware; it's easy put the cart before the horse.

- Fast by faith.

  Often, breakthroughs, receiving needed direction, and other spiritual benefits come only after fasting—sometimes much, much after. Don't let the enemy discourage you into thinking that your fast isn't accomplishing anything. Take any amount of opposition as encouragement to press on with all fervency. God rewards every fast done with godly intentions.

- Sustained personal revival and a fasted lifestyle go hand-in-hand.

  Study revival history, and you'll be hard pressed to find revivalists who didn't incorporate seasons of fasting into their prayer lives. Almost every great move of God has been birthed in prayer and fasting. Living a fasted lifestyle is a must if you want to experience nonstop personal revival and the power of God in your ministry.

THE DIRE NECESSITY OF AN INTERCESSORY PRAYER TEAM

In addition to having a vibrant prayer life as a woman in ministry, you also need intercessors to cry out to God on your behalf. I received this revelation through a prophetic word a few years before God launched me into the ministry. I was working as a high school teacher in a Christian school.

The school secretary, who operates in the gift of prophecy, approached me one day in the hallway. She told me that because God's call on my life was going to come to pass soon, I needed personal intercessors to provide me with a prayer covering. She said, "Proactively ask God for an intercessory prayer team. He'll provide."

I took her prophetic word seriously and asked God to supply the need. A few months later, my friend, JoAnn Kates, informed me of an encounter she had with the Lord. She joyfully proclaimed that while she was in prayer, God commanded her, "Pray for Jamie Morgan until you take your last breath." JoAnn had no prior knowledge that I had prayed for personal intercessors.

Since that day, JoAnn has interceded for me daily—whenever I have a preaching engagement, as I write books, when I'm in the throes of battle, and as the Lord gives her pause. I couldn't fulfill my calling without JoAnn answering hers. As my chief personal intercessor, she has now trained a group of about a dozen other Christians who have agreed to form what I call my *prayer shield*. But it all began with one—JoAnn Kates.

History demonstrates the importance of prayer coverings. Father Daniel Nash preceded Charles Finney, the leader of the Second Great Awakening, into every city where Finney preached. Nash then interceded for Finney and his crusade so that, when Finney arrived in town, the spiritual ground had already been tilled. Church history credits Nash as one of the reasons for Finney's great success.[18] Charles Finney had Father Nash. I have JoAnn Kates.

As a person called by God, you are automatically going to face greater attacks—new levels, new devils. That's just how it works, and that's just the way it is. Satan hates you and will do what he can to try to destroy your ministry and your walk with the Lord. You are like the leader of a battalion in the army of God. This automatically places a bullseye squarely on your back. If the enemy can take you down, he can also wipe out all those you influence in ministry.

In his book, *Prayer Shield*, C. Peter Wagner states, "Make no mistake about it: The higher you go on the ladder of Christian Leadership, the higher you go on Satan's hit list. Satan is more specific, persistent and intentional when it comes to pastors and leaders."

Because you are on the front lines,
you need a prayer shield.

You also need extra prayer support because great wisdom, discernment, strategy, strength, and energy is required for the ministry. The Apostle Paul asked for prayer support from the churches he provided with leadership at least eight times. He knew he couldn't do it without the prayers of other believers petitioning the Lord on his behalf.

The crux of the matter is this: The greater the prayer coverage, the greater your ministry effectiveness, and the more protected you'll be from the onslaught of the enemy's attacks. The lesser the prayer coverage, the less effective your ministry, and the more vulnerable you'll be to the fiery darts of the evil one.

18 J. Paul Reno, *Daniel Nash 1775-1831 Prayer Warrior for Charles Finney*, accessed April 14, 2018. https://hopefaithprayer.com/prayer-warrior-charles-finney/.

To raise up a prayer shield, begin like I did—with prayer. God will do for you what He did for me. He wants you to have abundant prayer coverage more than you do. Ask Him.

After you lift your need for personal intercessors before the Lord, look around you. Who are the passionate prayer warriors in your life? Who has a heart for your ministry? Who has shared that they pray for you? Make a list of those people.

With your list of potential prayer warriors in front of you, prayerfully ask yourself these questions: Whom can I trust? Who can keep a confidence? Who is a person of his or her word?

Through a process of elimination, since you'll share with your intercessory prayer team very personal information, struggles, and hurts, cross off your list those who can't be trusted with holding a confidence.

Also, eliminate those who aren't true to their word. If people promise to intercede for you daily, they need to pray for you daily. Some see the idea of being a part of an intercessory prayer team as spiritually romantic more than they like to do the work of prayer. Because of that, those who don't have a proven track record of faithfulness and commitment shouldn't be considered.

Next, take the remaining list before the Lord to inquire if any other names need to be deleted. Someone from outward appearances may check off all the boxes as the perfect intercessory team member, but God looks at the heart. If you don't have peace about someone on the list, cross that person off immediately. *"And let the peace that comes from Christ rule in your hearts"* (Colossians 3:15a). Don't try to figure it out, reason it out, or throw it out. The answer is simply, "No."

Now contact everyone on the list. Ask them if they would commit to praying for you every day for the next three months. Start with a junior varsity prayer team. When you contact them, clearly share the following so they know exactly what's expected and can make their decision accordingly.

- This is a commitment to be taken seriously.
- These are the things for which I need you to pray.
- Everything must be kept in the strictest of confidence.
- Please share anything with me that the Lord shows you.

At the end of the three-month period, evaluate if you want them to continue and ask them if they want to stay on the team of intercessors. Those who continue are now your official prayer shield. God will add to the team over time. Some won't stay for the duration. But in the long run, you'll have a solid prayer shield around you.

The strongest, most committed and passionate prayer warrior on the team will be your chief intercessor. This is the person to whom you'll communicate prayer requests, who will train and manage the team, and who will communicate back to you prophetic and directive messages from the team.

When the official prayer shield is formed, the intercession needs to go to the next level—a more strategic, intentional, and prophetic level. This will include spiritual warfare prayer (when the Lord identifies specific and targeted attacks and gives you a spiritual battle strategy for victory) and watchman prayer (praying while watching like the watchman on the wall of Jerusalem). While most praying will be done individually, I also highly suggest times of corporate prayer with the entire intercessory prayer team when possible.

Because forming a prayer shield for you and your ministry is utterly essential, I want to suggest the following books for further study.

- *Prayer Shield*—C. Peter Wagner
- *Praying for Your Pastor*—Eddie Byun
- *Possessing the Gates of the Enemy*—Cindy Jacobs
- *Watchman, Watchman What of the Night*—Joy Parrott
- *Intercessors Discover Your Prayer Power*—Beth Alves, Tommi Femrite, Karen Kaufman
- *Daniel Nash: Prevailing Price of Prayer*—J. Paul Reno

Daniel Nash was faithful to pray for Charles Finney until the end of Finney's ministry. After that, Father Nash, still a man of prayer, pastored a small church until his death. It's said that when he went into the woods to pray, you could hear his travail from miles away. Nash was buried in a remote cemetery in northern New York near the Canadian border. His tombstone is still there today. On it is written:

Daniel Nash
A Man of Prayer

I want something like that said of me—Jamie Morgan, A Woman of Prayer. I'm sure you also want to leave a similar legacy.

CHAPTER 7

Friends, Peers, Mentors, and Protégés

WHEN MY SON was a teenager, he asked me a question regarding a friend he wanted to spend time with. Here is how our conversation went:

SON: Mom, may I go over to my friend's house?

ME: No. (His friend was ungodly.)

SON: Why?

ME: Because, *"Bad company corrupts good character"* (1 Corinthians 15:33).

SON: But I won't let his bad character rub off on me. I'll bring him closer to the Lord.

ME: *"Walk with the wise and become wise; associate with fools and get in trouble"* (Proverbs 13:20).

SON: But that won't happen to me!

ME: You aren't the exception to the rule, son. The people you surround yourself with today are who you'll become next year. Take a good look at your friendships, including this boy with whom you want to be friends. Are they Christlike? Are they who you want to become?

SON: Well, no . . ..

As Kingdom leaders, it's extremely important with whom we associate. Everything can rise or fall based on our relationships—which is why we must choose our associations wisely. The people we allow into our close circle will eventually determine who we become regardless of the convictions we had when we started. Their fingerprints will be on our lives and ministries.

There is great need for us to discuss the important topic of relationships. It remains critical for you to forge godly friendships. Great hurt can transpire from allowing destructive relationships in your life.

There is an unspoken rule often perceived in the ministry.

Rule: "Ministers can't have friends."

While that isn't true and must be resisted at all costs, I understand why the school of thought exists. Almost every minister has experienced immense hurt from people we thought we could trust and considered a "friend." That kind of pain from broken relationships causes devastating results and usually takes much time to heal.

Variations of the unwritten philosophy about ministers not having friends also exist, such as,

- You can't have friends in your church if you're on staff.
- You can't have friends who aren't in the ministry because they won't be able to relate.
- You can't have friends. Period. There is simply no one you can trust.

While wisdom must be employed regarding friendships formed within your church as well as friendships outside the ministry, it's not only possible to have friends as a minister but encouraged.

Woman of God, you MUST have friends! Let me say it another way. You can't NOT have life-giving friendships in your life.

You need close, trustworthy friends for encouragement, inspiration, accountability, emotional health, and . . . *fun*. You need friends in whom you can confide. You need friends with whom you can let your hair down and who will provide a soft place to land when needed. You sometimes need a sounding board and a shoulder to cry on. You also need friends who will both confront you when you are headed for danger and spur you on to greater things in God.

God has created a system called the *body of Christ*. As a body of believers, we need each other. There are times I need you, and there are other times you need me. It's both unrealistic and unbiblical to think we don't need friendships. As a matter of fact, studies have shown that a key to ministerial longevity is having godly friends. And here is the reason:

Isolation leads to *desolation*.

If your life is void of friends, the enemy can make your life a barren wasteland. Leaders in ministry all too often isolate themselves for a variety of reasons. They do so because of a fear of getting hurt, the time constraints of ministry (little time for relationship building), lack of peer support, and so forth. Nonetheless, regardless of the reason, whenever isolation occurs it will lead to an unhealthy spiritual life and ministry.

You need three kinds of friends. You need your spouse (if you're married). You need peer relationships with those in the ministry. And you need friends outside of the ministry.

Yes, if you're married, your husband should be your closest friend. But he can't be your *only* friend. First, it puts too much pressure and unrealistic expectations on your spouse that he can't possibly live up to. Second, your husband may feel just as isolated and just as lonely as you do. You and your husband need to be each other's best friends, but you both need other friendships.

Ministry friendships are also crucial because you need friends you can bounce ministry-related ideas off of. You need friends from whom you can glean needed wisdom regarding conflict and challenges. And you need friends to sometimes talk you off the ministry ledge. They can pray for you from a shared vantage point, check your spiritual pulse, and speak the truth in love to you.

But you also need, yes, *girlfriends*. These are women outside of the ministry with whom you'll laugh, cry, go to dinner, take girls' weekends, and just do life. I have five female friends who fit in this category of friendship. We celebrate each other's birthdays and achievements, pray for each other's families, and support one another through difficulties. Woman of God, although you are a high-capacity leader, you are also a *woman*. You need friends, because you are a human being.

Of course it's important to make the distinction between friendship and ministry. When I'm friends with people, I give into the relationship, and they give into the relationship. I give. They give. I give. They give—and on and on. *Friendships are reciprocal relationships*. But when a relationship is ministry, I give. I give. I give. I give. And I don't receive or expect anything in return. When it comes to ministry, my expectation is completely in the Lord. *Ministry is a one-sided relationship.*

I'm convinced that it's crucial to differentiate between friendship and ministry, because there have been times when I've entered into what I thought was a friendship and was left disappointed because I was the only one giving into that relationship. That isn't a friendship. It's a relationship with someone who needs ministry.

But regardless of the types of friendships we form with others, it's paramount that we allow every relationship in our lives to be defined by God and not be based on our own expectations or the expectations of others.

HOW TO SELECT GODLY FRIENDS

Just like we should allow God to lead us to our spouses, churches, and the geographic locations where we live, He also should be allowed to lead us to our close friends. You will recognize the friends God has handpicked for you by the Spirit of God. Great discernment and listening to the voice of God are essential to choosing the right friends.

It's important to note the methods by which God sends to you the friends He has chosen for you. Sometimes *you find them*, and other times *they find you*. Just as God desires to direct your path, God will also direct the people He assigned to you for friendships. And sometimes the friends God directs your way arrive before you even know you needed that friendship.

Sometimes we find favor, and at other times favor finds us.

But beware. Someone may on the surface seem to check off all the "friend" boxes, but only God knows his or her heart, motives, and future decisions.

It cannot be overstated that entering into a close friendship without having heard from the Lord can waste time, have devastating consequences, and become a snare of the enemy.

The same principles apply when God wants to remove a friend from your life. Some friendships are for a lifetime, while others are for a season. As painful as it is to put space between you and a good friend, God knows best, and we follow the leading of God's Spirit in those times, too.

Here are five guidelines to assist you in selecting close, godly friends.

1. Choose only the friends who can see God's call on your life. Prior to God launching me into the ministry, I had three very close Christian friends. We were all young wives and mothers and walked through the Christian life together. I really valued those friendships.

One morning while in prayer, the Lord instructed me to distance myself from them. He said, "The Jamie they see is the Jamie that is standing before them. They can't see the Jamie you are going to be. Because their opinion of you matters to you, you must distance yourself. If you stay in close association, it will thwart my call on your life. It will ultimately hinder you from seeing yourself through my eyes."

I was devastated. "How can I possibly extricate myself from these dear friends?" I thought. I am ashamed to say that I obeyed God only two-thirds of the way. I managed to distance myself from two of those friends. But I couldn't bring myself to end my friendship with the third friend.

But out of His mercy, God did for me what I couldn't do—or *wouldn't* do. He ended my relationship with the third friend. She did something extremely hurtful to me. Oh how painful the incident was!

It would have been much less painful had I obeyed God. I'm eternally grateful that God had His way despite my outright disobedience. It's paramount that your friends see the call of God on your life, or else it will hinder you in more ways than you can count.

2. Choose friends who are secure in who they are in Christ. This is especially true if you are called to do great exploits for the Lord. The insecurity of a close friend can cause jealousy, rivalry, or control to rear its ugly head. Friends with insecurity issues want everyone to think well of them and are driven to be liked. They crave your attention and look for signs you might be disappointed in them. This can cause you to walk on eggshells when in their company.

The root of insecurity is pride. When people are prideful, their eyes are on themselves—whether they think of their value as too much, or too little. This doesn't make for a good friendship. The words *pride* and *friend* do not occupy the same space for too long.

Also, shame usually lurks in the background of the insecure person. Shame is known as the silent killer of relationships because it's hidden. It causes the person who suffers from it to feel unworthy, and that fuels *approval addiction*. Shame inhibits a person from being in healthy relationships. At the least, insecure friends will be high maintenance, and at the most, their friendship will be destructive.

But when the identities of your friends are firmly rooted in Christ, they will rejoice with you. They will cheer and champion you on when God does big things in your ministry. They won't be threatened by your ministry victories but will sincerely celebrate God's goodness to you.

They will also not fall apart if you don't give them the attention they deeply desire when your attention is elsewhere. They will expect nothing from you but appreciate everything.

Friends who are secure in the Lord
provide relationships filled with peace.

---

3. **Choose friends who are strong in faith.**

One of the miracles of Jesus is found in Mark 2:1–12. It contains the account of the healing of the paralyzed man in Capernaum. This miracle happened as the man's friends lowered him through a hole they made in the roof of the house where Jesus was ministering. They couldn't get him through the front door but still found a way to get him to Jesus. These are the types of friends with whom to surround yourself—people with BIG faith in our BIG God.

Select and keep friends who exhibit compassion when you are in need, encourage you when you're weak, and take you to Jesus through intercession. You want friends who know Jesus has all the answers and in fact *IS* the answer as they point you to Jesus when facing challenges and struggles. And, in turn, you need to do the same for them.

Honestly, we all struggle to not place limitations on God. Therefore, we must surround ourselves with those who also work hard at not putting limits on God. Those types of friends will call out our doubts and unbelief, admonish us to raise high our shields of faith, and believe God with us for miracles.

4. **Choose friends who are spiritually mature, wise in the Lord, and exhibit the character of Christ.**

Friends with these traits, while not perfect, are those who generally abide in the Vine, who exhibit the fruit of the Spirit, and who will be loyal, honest, and trustworthy. They will give you advice from the Word and not from the world. They're much more likely to walk in the Spirit and not in the flesh. Their insatiable hunger for the Word of God, unquenchable thirst for prayer, and passion for souls will sharpen and spur you on to greater works in Christ.

While spiritually mature friends will encourage you to take more territory for the Kingdom, they also won't expect you to be perfect. Some people are shocked to find out Kingdom leaders make mistakes, have weaknesses, and need mercy just like they do. While they have head knowledge that no one is perfect but Jesus, in practice, the spiritually immature often can't handle that truth.

Select friends who give you both space and grace to be human and don't have unrealistic expectations of you as a ministry leader. Surround yourself with people who treat you as a sister in Christ and who will love you unconditionally even when you're having a bad day.

Spiritually mature friends won't expect you to always be "on the job." This means they will allow you to discuss topics other than church and ministry and take a genuine interest in your personal life. It also means someone else can say grace over the meal (other than you). These are friends who see the *whole* of your life and not just a *part*.

And, finally, regarding peer-level ministry friends,

5. **Choose most peer friendships from the same stream—but also a few from different streams.**

Jesus said, *"Rivers of living water will flow from his heart"* (John 7:38b). Rivers have channels. Tell me, what channel is the anointing flowing through in your life? Find that channel of the Spirit and flow with ministry friends who have that same anointing. You will learn from each other and see both of your ministries increase.

Having said that, it's also advisable at times to associate with those from other channels—other anointings, denominations, five-fold ministry offices, regions, and so forth. I believe God wants us to cross-pollinate like bees that do the work of pollination in new fields.

While Kingdom alignment is crucial, multiplied revelation, giftings, and effectiveness await when we learn from brothers and sisters serving in areas of the harvest field with which we are not familiar. Occasionally stepping into spheres of ministry influence other than our own to learn, grow, and fellowship pleases the Lord and is necessary for our optimal effectiveness.

Sadly, though, I must warn you about "climbers"—those who will try to befriend you with ulterior motives. Be on guard regarding that type of peer association. "Climbers" want proximity to your position in order to "climb" the ministry ladder themselves. And once they have what they were after all along, they will drop you like a hot potato.

Please understand that God brings people into your life, but so does the enemy. Great discernment is needed when it comes to forming friendships. Only God knows the motives of our hearts. Therefore, it's only through the guidance of the Holy Spirit that you'll be able to distinguish a true ministry friend from a "climber." So please be aware.

MENTORS AND PROTÉGÉS

Another type of relationship that is crucial to pursue is *mentor-protégé* and *protégé-mentor* relationships. Every woman called to ministry should both have a mentor and be a mentor to someone else. A mentor pours into us. And in turn, we pour into others. An inlet with no outlet equals the Dead Sea.

Mentoring can be found in both the Old and New Testaments.

Moses mentored Joshua.

Naomi mentored Ruth.

Elijah mentored Elisha.

Barnabas mentored Paul.

Aquila and Priscilla mentored Apollos.

Paul mentored Timothy.

Jesus mentored the Twelve Disciples.

Jesus—who is our role model for every matter of life—concentrated His ministry on the twelve, who then turned the world upside down for the Lord Jesus Christ. This speaks volumes to the importance and value of mentoring.

WHAT IS MENTORING?

Today the popular terms, *counseling*, *coaching*, and *mentoring* are often used interchangeably, but they're actually very different. The best way to define mentoring—an often misunderstood concept—is to contrast these three terminologies.

Counseling looks at the *past* to heal your present.

Coaching looks into the *future* to help you make and meet godly goals using motivation and accountability. Coaches usually don't give advice. Their primary technique is to ask pointed questions to help you discover your own answers.

Mentoring is *an ongoing relationship* between an experienced person and a less experienced person for the purpose of helping the one with less experience. Christian mentors are spiritual fathers or mothers who raise up spiritual sons and daughters. Mentors share wise counsel, encouragement, knowledge, and stories from life experience. Mentors have been there, done that, and can help their protégés navigate the ropes of life and ministry.

To further illustrate the differences, let's say that there's a spiritual ditch up ahead that needs to be avoided. This is how a *counselor*, *coach*, and *mentor* would each respond:

COUNSELOR: "Let's get you healed from the past ditches into which you fell."

COACH: "You've stated your goal is to avoid the ditch ahead. What are some steps you can take to circumvent that ditch?"

MENTOR: "I see a ditch ahead that you can't see. You need

to know it's there, because it will cause untold pain and waste a huge amount of time. Let me tell you a story about the time I fell into a ditch, how God rescued me, and the lessons He taught me through that ordeal to help you sidestep the ditch that lies ahead in your ministry."

God uses counseling and coaching
in various seasons of our lives,
but mentoring is for every season.

The essence of discipling is mentoring (standing in your own mentor's shadow while your protégés stand in yours). Therefore mentoring should span our entire lives and ministries.

When you find a mentor with whom you have ministry alignment (beliefs, core values, same ministry channel, similar anointing), you'll experience the acceleration of ministry. I'd heard people say this for years, but it wasn't until I had a mentor speaking into my life that my ministry exponentially increased in both reach as well as in effectiveness.

Prior to having a mentor, I did ministry alone, tried hard to figure most things out by myself, and lacked general support. But when I had mentors in my life, they helped me put the pieces of the puzzle together by imparting to me what they had been given. It's a genuine blessing both to be mentored and to mentor others.

ESTABLISHING A MENTORSHIP

The mentor can invite the protégé into a mentorship (like Jesus did the Twelve), or the protégé can approach the mentor and request guidance. I've seen both ways work successfully. Does it matter who does the initiating when God is involved in the relationship? If you ask someone to be either your mentor or your protégé, make sure you paint a picture of the why, what, when, and how of the relationship you are proposing.

Explain,

- Why you want the relationship.
- What you've seen in that person that made you want to enter the relationship.
- What you hope to gain by it.
- When you want to meet (once a week, once a month, etc.).
- How you want to meet (in person, online, phone, etc.).
- What mentoring goals you have.
- What mentoring methods you would like to use (book, Bible, questions and answers, doing ministry together, etc.).
- What timeframe you are proposing for the relationship (three-months, six-months, one-year, etc.). People are much more likely to enter into mentorship if there is a start and end date, although the mentorship can continue long after that—even for a lifetime.

BENEFITS OF HAVING A MENTOR

Of course you already know how strongly I feel about the value of mentoring, but let me add the following list of its benefits to define what I feel is to be gained by having a mentor (and what is to be gained by those you mentor too).

- Mentors affirm God's call on your life and give you much needed support.
- Mentors are concerned with your future, while others may focus on your past.
- Mentors will put you on the fast track of ministry and

catapult you into your destiny.

- Mentors will either promote or offend you. Your response to any and all correction they provide determines the outcome.
- Mentors are never content until every ounce of God's call on your life comes to pass.
- Mentors help you avoid disaster.
- Mentors help you see your blind spots and weaknesses.
- Mentors inspire, encourage, and challenge you to rise up and build higher.
- Mentors help to light your fire. They increase your passion and desire for ministry.
- Mentors make a lot of statements like, "If I were you . . .," "The mistakes I've made . . .," and, "Lessons I've learned . . .." Learning from their experiences has great benefits.
- Mentors will protect you and go to bat for you.
- Mentors will help release revelation, Holy Spirit creativity, and heavenly strategy.
- Mentors are tools in the hands of the Holy Spirit to mold, shape, and make you into who God is calling you to be.

A healthy mentor/protégé relationship occurs when the mentor has her protégé's absolute best interest at heart and wants her to accomplish more for the Lord than she ever dreamed possible. The mentor will encourage, correct, and rebuke with great patience and careful instruction (2 Timothy 4:2). Her motive will always be one of love even when saying difficult things.

In addition, the protégé postures herself to receive. She is teachable and correctable. (Please note that rebuke and correction are 2/3 of the equation.) My experience has been that some protégés *say* they want correction until you give it to them. But in real, life-giving mentor/protégé relationships, the protégé truly wants to be corrected—and even directly rebuked if necessary (though it never feels good at the time). She receives the correction, takes it before the Lord, and adjusts herself accordingly.

WARNING SIGNS IN THE PROCESS OF MENTORING

As in every bond between two people, a healthy, successful mentoring relationship can only continue when both parties in the relationship honor it and do everything they can to sustain it. Sometimes one of them fails in that effort, and usually it's the person being mentored. Here are the warning signs to watch out for to reveal your protégé has lost her passion to be mentored.

- She stops placing value on your wisdom.
- She displays resistance instead of willingness.
- She defends and makes excuses for herself (pride) when you bring her correction.
- She is a leaky bucket. She never gets around to applying what you've poured into her.
- She has stopped showing you honor and respect.
- She misses more than two meetings without a good excuse (no longer valuing your time).
- She frustrates you and debilitates your energy.

It would be a mistake to stay in a mentorship that exhibits any of these characteristics, especially if they are ongoing. When experiencing these things, perhaps it's time to tell your protégé, "I love you, but let's just be friends!" Sometimes mentorships are for a season, and you need to recognize when the season is over.

DISAPPOINTMENT

Before closing this chapter, our discussion on this topic wouldn't be complete without talking about disappointment. When you are discipling/mentoring others, some of the women you mentor may greatly disappoint you. That can come in the form of them dropping the ball, never getting around to applying what they learn, devaluing their mentorship with you, or maybe even their betrayal of your trust.

I've mentored for decades, and at one time or another in my ministry I've dealt with all of the warning signs I listed above. When it happens to you, you feel like you never want to mentor another human being as long as you live. That is the enemy trying to stop ministry multiplication from taking place through you.

Several years ago I found myself in one particular mentoring quandary. The protégé into whom I had poured myself fell into sin—*hard*. I was so disappointed at the poor choices she made. One day in prayer, after expressing my hurting heart to the Lord about the situation, He said to me, "Your reward in Heaven will not be based on the number of people your protégés reach. Your reward will be based on the number of people they would have reached had they applied all that you taught them and walked in the fullness of their calling."

God's perspective changes everything! Woman of God, please be cognizant of this. If Jesus' disciples fell asleep when He asked them to pray, some of the people you mentor probably will too! God will personally reward you for the cost and time you put forth in each mentoring relationship regardless of the outcome.

I stand by my conviction. Mentoring is one of the main instruments the Holy Spirit uses to make those called by God into vessels fit for the Master's use.

CHAPTER 8

Speaking: Tips, Tools, and Techniques

YOU ARE A Christian speaker.

Now *you* say it. "I am a Christian speaker."

Now say it like you mean it. "I AM a Christian speaker!"

Ok, now say it louder to make sure the devil hears you.

"I AM A CHRISTIAN SPEAKER!"

Oh, and by the way, this is what you're NOT: a motivational, inspirational, or self-improvement speaker who gives talks. While God will use your messages to *motivate* people to hunger after Him, *inspire* a passion for souls, or *improve* their prayer lives, such worldly titles and occupations have zero place in the life of a Kingdom leader.

You are a Christian speaker because you speak about Jesus. No matter the topic, Jesus is always the focus as well as the answer. Christianity is all about Jesus. The Bible is all about Jesus. And your speaking ministry should be all about Jesus.

True ministry is the ministry of Christ,
or it's no ministry at all.

Whew! Got that out of the way! Now, moving onward—

YOUR VOICE, GOD'S HEART

God needs your voice! Even if you aren't a pulpit minister, conference speaker, or Bible study and devotional leader, if you're a Christian, you're automatically a Christian speaker. Your voice communicates the gospel and the deep things of God's heart. In essence, you are God's megaphone. Your voice gives oral expression to God's message.

This implies you've spent consistent, quality time with Him developing intimacy of relationship to give Him the time, space, and availability to deposit His heart into yours. By the way, God only shares His heart with those He knows He can trust. Do you share the deep things of your heart with someone you can't trust? Of course not. And neither will God.

As a Christian speaker, you are to communicate what delights and pleases God. You articulate His plans, purposes, and pursuits. God will use your voice to set crooked paths straight, give needed direction, bring order amid chaos, and raise the dead to life. With holy boldness you'll proclaim the Word, the Name, and the Blood by the power of the Holy Spirit.

God needs your voice!

It doesn't matter if your voice is raspy, high-pitched, or so soft it's barely audible. I don't care if you're an extrovert, an introvert, stutterer, sputterer, or mutterer. GOD NEEDS YOUR VOICE. And this is the reason the enemy has tried to silence you with thoughts he injected into your mind, like, "No one wants to hear what you have to say." "You talk too loud." "You're not articulate enough." "So many people are better speakers than you." "You're just a woman."

Lies!

Regardless of your calling, your voice is integral. All excuses need to come off the table, including *FEAR*.

COMBATTING FEAR

Anyone out there ever battle the fear of public speaking?

Let me rephrase the question. Anyone *not* battle this fear?

The first time I spoke in front of an audience (besides the time I played Charlie Brown's sister in my elementary school play) was at my father's funeral. I had no intention of speaking, but God wanted me to communicate His heart to the lost souls in attendance. I was a new Christian and was learning up-close-and-personal what 2 Timothy 4:2 (NKJV) means by being ready "out of season."

In front of an audience of thirty, I stood behind that funeral home pulpit and presented the gospel. My voice quivered, my head throbbed from crying for days, and my body shook uncontrollably. But compelled by my love for Christ and passion for the lost, I pushed past the feeling of fear and did it.

There are many specific types of fears related to speaking in front of an audience, but here is a short list, and under each fear is God's corresponding solution.

- Fear: I'll be the center of attention.
  Solution: Die to self.
- Fear: I'll look like a fool.
  Solution: Die to self.
- Fear: I'm not good enough.
  Solution: Die to self.
- Fear: I'll make a mistake.
  Solution: Die to self.

- Fear: I won't know what to say.
  Solution: Die to self.

You get the point. *Self* is the root of fear. We experience fear when our eyes are fixed squarely on ourselves and not on Jesus. Being fully dead to self equals being fully alive in Christ.

ACCEPT OR NOT ACCEPT—THAT IS THE QUESTION

Ok, you open your email and there it is—an invitation to speak at a church, conference, retreat, or event. *Hip hip hooray!* I rejoice with you over God's goodness.

You're going to accept, *right*? Not so fast . . .

Please remember what I'm about to say to you as long as you live. Every open door is not from God.

Bam!

Some open doors are from God, but others lead to empty closets. And others, still, are traps from the enemy designed to lead to your demise. Regardless of your excitement, just because you received an invitation to speak doesn't mean you should accept it.

Following are the steps to take after you receive an invitation to speak.

1. Respond immediately (within 24 hours at the latest) to the person who sent you the invitation.
2. Profusely thank the host for the honor and inform him or her you'll pray over the invitation and get back soon with your response. And make sure you ask for the deadline for responding.
3. Gather from the host as much initial information as possible about the event. Ask for information like:

- Name and position of host (If he or she is not the senior leader, you need to know the host has authority to invite you.)

- Ministry website and social media handles
- Approximate number of attendees (This is so you're prepared with enough books, handouts, and so forth. You aren't going to make your decision to accept or decline based on this number—even though many speakers do. *Ugh!*)
- Statement of faith
- Event title, location, start and end times, and any other details
- Other speakers invited
- Closest airport if you must travel by air
- What the speaker budget is (Honorarium? Free will offering? While the decision to speak at the event should never be made based on money, it's good to discuss these details up front to avoid surprises.)
- What the host feels God wants to accomplish using the event
- What topic the host is requesting you to speak about
- How much time is allotted for you to speak (Your message should always be five minutes shorter than the time given. Example: If you're given 30 minutes, prepare your message to be 25 minutes long.)
- How the host heard about you

4. Pray. Lift all of the above in prayer before the Lord. Take as much time as you need within the deadline given—but obviously the sooner the better when it comes to responding.

5. After you've heard from the Lord, inform the host of your decision. If you accept, mark it in stone on your calendar and let nothing get in the way. If you decline, once again express gratefulness to the host for the invitation. As much as is possible with you, you want to maintain a good ministry relationship with others.

Following are some reasons why I've declined speaking invitations.

- The Lord said, "No." (Nuff said!)
- The event conflicted with other speaking engagements or family celebrations.
- The reason for the event was not one that aligned with my calling. (It's important to stay in your ministry lane.)
- The ministry hosting the event had doctrinal differences I didn't agree with and couldn't overlook.
- Another speaker at the event was someone of poor reputation or was known to live a life of compromise. (Please know that you'll forever be associated with the other speakers with whom you share an event platform. The internet never forgets!)
- Even though on paper everything about the event seemed right, I had turmoil in my spirit. (If you have turmoil, a check, or uneasiness in your spirit, don't try to reason it out in your head as to why you should accept the speaking invitation. Just say, "NO." Trust me, you'll be glad you did and regret if you don't!)

PRAYER—THE CRUCIAL FIRST STEP

Message preparation is sacred. It isn't less sacred than the sermon delivery. So many Christian speakers make the mistake of focusing more on the delivery than the steps leading up to the delivery. Yes, both the message preparation and delivery are equally sacred and need to be approached as such. And it all starts with prayer.

Prayer is the point of first-beginning in planning what you are going to say at any speaking engagement. Although this is fundamental, it's a step that mustn't be skipped. I emphasize this because many times people do skip it.

The moment you are asked to speak, start bathing the event in prayer. Even if the event is six months, or even one year out, start praying right away. Also, communicate to your intercessory prayer team that you've accepted an invitation to speak, and include all the pertinent details so they can begin praying as well. Hearing from God takes time lingering in His presence. *Speaking for* God begins and ends with *listening to* God.

First, ask God to prepare your heart. Message preparation must be approached with a ready heart. The Holy Spirit needs to do a deep work in your heart before transformation can happen in the hearts of the people to whom you'll be ministering. A message anointed by the Holy Spirit flows out of your heart and not your head. Therefore, your heart needs to be clean and filled with the power of the Holy Spirit and the love of Christ. This applies whether you are presenting a "hallelujah–type" sermon or a hard, corrective-type message.

Without prayer as the foundation, what differentiates your message from any speech given at your local Rotary Club? Prayer is the difference between an anointed sermon delivered from the heart and a dry speech given from the head.

Next, pray for God to give you a burden for the people to whom you are ministering. (Your message subject will be determined later.) If you don't have that burden, the people will sense your lack of passion. God is burdened for them. He is also clearly burdened for the biblical theme you'll be presenting. But you can't speak with authority if you aren't burdened for your audience.

Then ask God what topic He wants you to address. Even if the host has given you a specific topic, there are various approaches and directions you can take. There are topics within topics. For example, the host may have given you the topic of "marriage" for a couples conference. Will your message be "Healing for Troubled Marriages" or "Strengthening Marriages"? You may have been presented a plane to land, but there are many different runways on which to land that plane.

So take all the information you gathered from the host regarding the event before the Lord. (This is yet another reason why it's important to collect those details.) Lay it all out before Him in prayer. Pray in tongues. Begin making a list of thoughts that come to mind on a piece of paper. Keep praying over the topic, adding any additional topics as they arise.

Now pray over the list you've made. Often you'll have a knowing in your knower the direction God wants you to take. But until you do, keep praying.

Sometimes God will give you an inkling—a small glimpse—of the direction in which to head. And as I've said before, a rock that's rolling is easier to move and direct than a boulder that's stationary. So begin going in the direction you feel inclined to go, but keep checking your spirit the entire time.

In other words, don't pray about direction and then curl up on the couch to watch your favorite television show. Start studying in the direction you think God wants you to go. Keep praying. And He will lead you from there.

Lastly, invite the Holy Spirit into the sacred work of message preparation. Ask Him to guide you, to anoint you, and to change you as you are preparing the sermon. Give the Holy Spirit full access to your heart and mind. Posture yourself for Him to pour into you so you can then pour into the people to whom you've been entrusted to speak—to all those whom He dearly loves.

KEYS TO MESSAGE PREPARATION

Location, Location, Location. While this is a popular real estate term, it's also pertinent to preparing God's messages. Where do you have the least distractions, hear God the best, and find yourself the most able to be creative? Would your office be ideal, or perhaps a coffee shop, public library, or park bench? Prepare your messages in a place that works best for you.

The time of day is just as relevant. What hour of the day do you accomplish the most, think the clearest, and have the highest energy? We don't perform well when we're tired or when our thinking is fuzzy. Therefore, we owe it to the people to whom we are ministering to prepare messages during a time when we can achieve maximum impact.

Ok, you've situated yourself at the location and time most conducive to preparing your message. You have your Bible, study books, notebook, laptop computer, and pen in tow. But how do you start? Before you open your laptop, you must come to the place of message study with these absolute convictions:

- The Bible is the very Word of God.
- It's inspired by the Holy Spirit.
- It's perfect and infallible (unable to fail).
- It's living and active.
- It's the primary way God speaks.
- As I study God's Word I listen to the Holy Spirit.
- As I listen, the Holy Spirit will speak.
- I'll speak to my audience what I hear Him say.
- God's Word and the power of the Holy Spirit will transform their lives.

This may seem fundamental, but it can't be overstated. No matter how many years you've prepared and delivered messages, these convictions must be in the forefront of your mind and planted deep within your heart. Please don't ever forget them. If you do, you'll lean less and less on God and more and more on yourself.

(*God forbid!*) Unfortunately, it happens to some Christian speakers every day.

The Word of God is the diamond of your message. Your points, illustrations, and other parts of your delivery must be like the setting of a ring. Their purpose is to showcase the diamond. And Scripture itself is the centerpiece of every message you'll ever deliver, because its purpose is to display Jesus.

Now, let's focus on some details of message preparation.

Using a concordance, make a list of Scriptures on the topic God has given you for the message. Prayerfully begin reading each one to determine the passage the Lord highlights for the purpose of the message. His anointing is obviously on every verse in the Bible, but which passage do you sense His anointing on for such a time as this? That is the passage you'll choose.

Now you're going to dig, dig, dig into that biblical text like an archeologist digs for precious artifacts. What a joy and honor to study God's Word! Here is the process I use to study the Scripture passage for my messages: *Read, Observe, Interpret, and Apply.*

Read

1. Pray for revelation, insight, and understanding.
2. Pace the floor or ground and pray in tongues. (I'm a pacer.)
3. Read the passage in the translation from which you're preaching.
4. Pace and pray in tongues.
5. Read the passage out loud again and again, each time emphasizing a different word.
6. Pace and pray in tongues.
7. Read the passage in other translations.
8. Pace and pray in tongues.

9. Read the entire chapter in which the passage appears for context. Now read the whole book where the Scripture is located.
10. Pace and pray in tongues.

Observe

After reading, praying, reading, and praying, your study of the Bible text must begin with what God was saying to the original audience—such as the First Century followers. Only then can we interpret what He's saying to us—the Twenty-first Century followers. (We'll talk more about this in the next step.)

Put on your Holy Spirit detective glasses and list all the things you observed from the *Read* steps you just took. Jot down everything you learned and what the Holy Spirit illuminated for you. Once you feel you've dug out of the mine everything you possibly can, dig deeper still. Following is a list of questions to help you do that. Add to your ongoing observations list the answers to the questions.

- Who penned this book?
- To whom was the author writing?
- Who are the people mentioned in the book?
- What is the major theme or focus of the book?
- What were the main events recorded in the book?
- Why was there a need for this to be written?
- Did the author use key or repeated words? What are they?
- Were there any historical customs or cultural references noted to research?
- Are there any figures of speech or biblical idioms that need to be defined?

Once you've made your own observations, then (and only then) consult commentaries, study Bibles, Bible software, and other reference material. I repeat—*then and only then*. It's of the utmost importance you don't use study aids until you've heard from God yourself.

While study aids prove helpful, they're based on what the authors of those study aids have observed and heard from God (second-hand hearing). Before turning to other resources, always give the Holy Spirit the opportunity to communicate with you first through the Word, prayer, and personal study.

Interpret

In this step you'll determine what God is saying through the passage to today's hearer—to you, the present-day Church, and our world today. On another page, write down the answers to the following questions regarding the biblical passage you are studying.

- What did I learn about God?
- How can I grow in greater intimacy to God with what I've learned?
- What did I learn about people?
- How can I better minister to people with what I've learned?
- Is there a command to obey?
- Is there a sin to avoid?
- Is there a promise to claim?
- Is there an example to follow?
- What are the biblical principles in this passage?
- How can I look more like Jesus because of this passage? (The ultimate goal.)

Apply

Here is where you're going to pull it all together for your audience. Lift everything up in prayer—everything you've observed and heard the Lord say regarding the passage. Ask God, "What do you want to say to the people?"

Write down what you believe God is saying to you. Then ask yourself the question of questions. **In one sentence, what does God want to say to my audience?**

Your answer to this ONE sentence will become the "overarching point" of your message. In academic circles it's called the thesis. Sometimes it's referred to as the "sticky statement," "big idea," or "takeaway." The overarching point will be repeated in various ways throughout your message.

Every message has an overarching point—that ONE point. (Did I say just ONE?) That ONE point is what God wants the audience to remember. Gone are the days of the six-point sermons. Oh, pastors still deliver them, but the people remember just ONE thing he or she says. What ONE thing does God want your audience to remember through your message?

To demonstrate the principle of the "overarching point," let's pretend you leave church one Sunday, stop at the grocery store, and bump into a family who didn't make it to church (another sermon for another day). "What was pastor's sermon about today?" they ask. What is the ONE thing you'll tell them about the message? That thing was the ONE thing you remembered, and hopefully it was the overarching point of your pastor's message.

To further illustrate, I'm going to list a series of six numbers: 24, 86, 12, 71, 3, 789. Now without looking, repeat these numbers back to me. (Don't peek!) Most likely you can't.

Let's try it again. Here is another list: 78, 78, 78, 78, 78, 78. Now repeat this list back to me. I'm sure you could do it this time around. This proves the very reason for focusing on and reinforcing the overarching point.

One of the 1,000-plus messages I've preached over my ministry lifetime was on the topic of *perseverance*. For that sermon, God gave me this overarching point: "If you don't quit, you win!" I stated this in the beginning of the message and sprinkled it liberally throughout. It even became the title to the sermon.

That was years ago, but to this day people who heard that message will still say to me, "I'll never forget something you said. If you don't quit, you win!" They've even relayed instances when they were tempted to throw in the towel, but in that moment, God brought back to their recall, "If you don't quit, you win!" And it caused them to persevere.

Now all your hard work of prayer and Bible study will come together in the form of an outline. This is what you'll take up with you to the pulpit or speaker's podium. You obviously won't pack into your message everything you've learned, only those things the Holy Spirit leads you to share. And the outline simply organizes what He has spoken to you. Here is a sample outline.

Title

(Establish a title that is both appealing AND clearly relevant.)

I. Scripture Passage

II. Introduction

III. Overarching Point (Reveal the focus of the message.)

IV. An explanation of what God was saying to the original hearer (This is what you discovered in the "Observe" step of your study.)

V. Overarching Point (Restate the overarching point.)

VI. An explanation of what God is saying to the present-day Church and the world today (This is the results of your study's "Interpret" step.)

VII. Overarching Point (Restate the overarching point.)

VIII. An explanation of what God is saying to us (This is the results of the "Apply" step.)

IX. Overarching Point (Bring it home; end by restating the overarching point.)

X. Altar Call and closing (Ask the host if he or she wants you to give the altar call, but come prepared to do it.)

As you complete your message outline, picture three people sitting in chairs across from you—an unsaved person, a new believer, and a mature believer. In most audiences (unless told otherwise) all three types of people are present and need to be reached. Keeping all three people in mind, be cognizant of the language, expressions, and illustrations you use. This will ensure you'll impact everyone in the audience regardless of spiritual condition or maturity level.

Now practice, practice, practice. Try to memorize the opening, closing, and overarching point. Even practice not being afraid of their faces, which was something God told Jeremiah not to do after He gave Jeremiah a hard message of repentance to preach (Jeremiah 1:8). Speak what God gives you whether the countenances of your listeners are happy, sad, mad, or glad. Fear God, not man.

MESSAGE DELIVERY AND PULPIT MANNERS

In closing this chapter I leave you with a list of things you should do every time you are invited to speak.

- Arrive thirty minutes earlier than what you were instructed.
- Be prepared to give the media team your list of Scriptures, *PowerPoints*, and any other media aids you want to use.

- Get alone with God before the service and empty yourself of *you* (fear, insecurity, flesh, pride, doubt, etc.). Ask God to fill you to overflowing with His Spirit.
- When you're introduced, spring up right away and approach the pulpit with confidence in your every step.
- If using a handheld microphone, hold it a fist-length distance from your mouth. And when using a headset, make sure you don't wear earrings that make a clanging sound. The earring noise will be heard in the audio and visual recording as well as the live feed.
- The first words you'll say from the pulpit will be used to thank the host for inviting you to speak and entrusting you with his or her pulpit.
- Never, ever, tell the audience how nervous you are (even if you are). The confidence you exhibit will be the confidence with which they will receive your message.
- Begin making eye contact right away. Divide the audience into thirds. Look to the right, then middle, then left, then middle, then right, then middle, and continue doing so during your entire delivery.
- As much as is possible, stand to the left and to the right of the pulpit. The pulpit can create a barrier between you and the audience, and insecure speakers will often use it to hide behind.
- If you make a mistake (you will—everyone does), adjust yourself and just keep going.
- Change your speaking pace. Say some things fast and others slowly. Every so often take a dramatic pause, especially after saying something impactful.
- Involve the audience as much as possible. For example, say something like, "Repeat after me . . .," or, "Naboth stood

up to Ahab! Let's all give him a handclap!" or, "It began to rain on Noah's Ark. Everyone tap your hand using only one finger" (together it makes the sound of light rain).

- Don't use words that border on vulgarity, even if they're commonly used in today's vernacular. If you do, you'll alienate an entire demographic of people and prevent them from receiving your message. They'll stop listening after you say that questionable word, phrase, or example.
- Be as real, transparent, and authentic as possible. Tell on yourself. Joke about yourself.
- Before you leave the speaking engagement, profusely thank the host for inviting you.
- Within three days after the event, mail the host a thank you note (or send a text message).

Speaking for God is one of the greatest honors in the world! The Holy Spirit will lead and guide your every step. Pray much, study hard, and open your mouth. He will fill it!

CHAPTER 9

Trade Secrets for Traveling Ministers

JESUS HAD A traveling ministry. His apostles did as well. God may be calling you to travel to make His name famous. Many women in ministry are involved in some sort of traveling ministry—whether full-time, part-time, or on occasion. God opens doors for five-fold ministers, music minsters, missionaries, Bible study leaders, and testimony-givers to *"Go into all the world and preach the Good News to everyone"* (Mark 16:15).

It's my personal belief that regardless of our callings we should be prepared to GO, whether to a nearby town or a nation across the ocean. I feel so strongly about this that I think every believer should own a passport. I want to be ready in season and out of season. He bids me GO, so I GO! I am prepared to fully obey, no questions asked.

There are many intricacies involved in the traveling ministry. To some it appears mysterious; to others it looks like a hard life; and still to others it seems glamorous. But while traveling for Jesus is neither glamorous nor mysterious, it abounds with the grace of God. When you're obeying what God has called you to do, though at times it may be difficult, there is joy unspeakable.

I absolutely love the traveling ministry. I love everything about it—air travel, meeting new people, experiencing new cultures (inside and outside my nation), and of course new opportunities to advance the Kingdom. I love getting away from the familiar, and I love coming home. Both give me fresh perspectives.

Chapter eight addressed accepting an invitation, message prep, and pulpit manners when invited to speak, but the purpose of this chapter is to equip you for ministry travel (now or in the future) and give you the wisdom needed to be an effective road warrior for Jesus!

I've divided the trade secrets of traveling ministry into six different categories. They are the six keys to effective traveling ministry—*communication*, *organization*, *avoiding appearances of evil*, *relationship building*, *faith for finances*, and a *servant's heart*. Some wisdom nuggets are extremely spiritual, while others are intensely practical. Both kind are needed for successful ministry on the road.

COMMUNICATION

You're getting ready for your next ministry trip. It's so exciting to think of all the God-possibilities that exist—souls saved, signs and wonders in abundance, hearts healed, and God's Spirit poured out. But there is much preparation to be done before the travel day arrives.

The first thing to ask yourself is this: Does anything need to be communicated to the host (pastor, conference organizer, etc.)? This is the time to get your questions answered, clear up any gray areas of your trip, and talk about everything in advance. I'm a huge proponent of the principle, "Let's talk about it now before it actually happens."

Eliminating the element of surprise is crucial for your speaking event to go as smoothly as possible. You could give the enemy a foothold if there is misunderstanding or confusion. Ultimately, you need to be on the same page as the host. You are the guest in someone's spiritual home, and it's the rules of that house to which you must abide.

Therefore, ask and discuss the following beforehand.

- **Are you arranging my air travel and hotel?**

  Sometimes the host does; other times it's you. Most speakers want to arrange their own airfare and hotel because of brand loyalty as well as earning points for future ministry travel. Either way, this is nothing that can be assumed but must be verified well in advance of your trip.

  By the way, it's always preferable to arrive the day before you are scheduled to speak. This will ensure you're punctual and that you are well rested before your time of ministry. I book my hotel when I accept the speaking engagement (notating confirmation code and cancellation policy) and purchase the airfare approximately one month before the trip.

- **Who is picking me up at the airport?**

  First, it's important to ask this question to make sure someone is picking you up. A minister friend recently told me the host expected her to get from the airport to the event by herself. That should never be. Second, it's important to make sure it's not a man alone who is picking you up at the airport to take you to your hotel. (I'll go into this in greater detail below.) And it's also important to receive the person's cell phone number before you leave for the trip. Send a text message to the person as soon as you land and ask where he or she is waiting.

- **May I have a product table?**

  Most hosts will gladly oblige this request, but others don't for their own personal reasons. If the host allows it, ask if a table will be supplied. Don't assume even the smallest of details.

- **May I collect the email addresses of your congregation at my product table?**

  A growing e-mail list is essential to a growing ministry these days. Explain to the host why you want to ask church members to share with you their email addresses (for use with monthly newsletters, travel schedules, promotions, etc.) and then leave the decision with him or her. Some pastors have had nightmare experiences with guest speakers who split the church by contacting members after the event and enticing them to attend their own church. Because of this, there will be a contingency who won't give you permission. But ask, because most will.

- **May I talk about my ministry, products, or projects from the pulpit?**

  One of the roles of a pastor is to protect the vision of the church and some may view your ministry as a competing vision. Most will allow it, however, but make sure you ask.

- **How should I dress?**

  It's crucial to honor the culture of the house. The modes of dress in some places of ministries in which you'll speak are jeans and sneakers, while in other places they are dresses and high heels. The church I pastored was extremely casual in dress. One time we had a guest speaker who arrived in a suit and tie. I could tell the people weren't receiving his ministry; he intimidated them with his formal style of dress. The speaker noticed it too, took off his suit jacket, and made a joke about not ironing the back of his shirt. They laughed and immediately began receiving from him. Find out what the culture is and dress accordingly.

- **Your diet.**

  Every traveling minister knows it's extremely difficult to always eat healthy meals while traveling. Restaurant meals, eating at odd hours, the lack of options, being away from the familiar, and celebrating what God has done with fatty desserts can lead to an unhealthy temple. This is particularly true if you travel frequently. While most restaurants have healthy options on their menu to choose from, if you follow a particular plan of eating, that too should be communicated to the host beforehand. My suggestion is to include something like this in your ministry confirmation email: "Dr. Jamie Morgan is frequently asked what type of food she prefers. To make your planning and preparation for her visit easier, here is the food plan she follows . . .."

- **Your honorarium.**

  There are two prevalent schools of thought regarding speaker offerings. (1) Have a set fee, or (2) Don't mention money at all (you get what you get). While I don't have a set fee, I've been the recipient of "a mug and a hug" honorarium, so I understand why some ministers do set fees. Every minister must follow her personal conviction regarding this issue. Although I address more on the topic of finances below, a middle-of-the-road approach might be to provide a range for a suggested honorarium. Many times the host will bring up the subject, but if they don't, you could also include this topic in your email confirmation. For instance, "I'm working out the travel logistics for Dr. Jamie Morgan. She is frequently asked about her speaking fees. Although she doesn't have a set fee, here is a suggested honorarium range: from $_______ to $_______."

ORGANIZATION

Organization is key to an efficient traveling ministry. This can't be over-emphasized.

Even if you aren't a natural organizer, learn this needed skill. Without organization, your travel preparation will take twice as long and will make your itinerant stay more cumbersome than it needs to be.

Think in terms of having a second home. When people have a second home, they need some (not all) of the same items they have at their main residence. Wherever you travel, it's your second home—your home away from home. This is one of the reasons most traveling ministers have airline and hotel brand loyalty (besides earning points). It gives them a sense of familiarity and sameness while they are away from home.

The first organizational tip I want to share is the old adage, *a place for everything, and everything in its place*. Store your luggage in a specific location of your home. It should be a spot that is out of the way yet a place from where your luggage can be quickly retrieved when packing for a trip. When you come home after a ministry engagement, put your luggage back in the designated place whether you feel like it or not. Remember, *A place for everything, and everything in its place.*

Store travel items inside your luggage (airplane neck pillow, jewelry organizer, travel-sized plastic bottles, etc.) so all you'll need to do is unzip your suitcase and they're at your disposal. Store in it a travel set of toiletries, make-up bag, breath mints for altar ministry (the wind of God shouldn't smell), phone/laptop chargers, tote bag—all that's needed for travel. That way, all you'll need to add to your suitcase are your clothes, shoes, and jewelry.

Included on my list of things to do in preparation for my trip is to purchase the host a thank-you gift. My favorite gifts to present to express my gratefulness for the speaking invitation is personalized stationery embossed with his or her name or a gift certificate to a favorite restaurant (check with the host's administrative assistant for restaurant suggestions). These types of thank-you presents indicate that thought was put into the gift. A small gift may be also purchased for the host's spouse, if appropriate.

When selecting clothing to pack for your trip, think in terms of complete outfits—top, pants, shoes, jewelry, belt, scarf, and watch—for each day. Place all accessories for one outfit in a bag and label it, for example, "Friday's outfit." (As a side note, I also do the same with my vitamins.) This grab-n-go system makes for efficient travel.

If you're traveling the same day as your scheduled speaking engagement, wear the outfit for travel that you plan to speak in. Always assume you won't have time to change at your hotel; but if you do it's a bonus.

Many traveling ministers will recount for you all the occasions their suitcases were lost by airlines. So, many now fit everything for travel in their carry-on suitcase. Watch online videos recorded by experienced globetrotters on how to pack your carry-on with the greatest efficiency and least wrinkles. You'll get better and better at this the more practiced you are.

It's advisable to make a travel checklist. Make multiple copies of it, and store them inside your luggage. That way you don't have to make a list every time you travel and suffer from the "I feel like I forgot something" syndrome.

In addition to the items needed for travel, also include household action items you need to take care of before you leave, such as doing chores, paying bills, making phone calls, watering plants, boarding a pet, getting a manicure, and so forth. When preparing for travel these items are as important as the articles you pack.

When you arrive at your destination hotel, unpack right away. Hang your clothes up and press any that need ironing. Place your toiletries in the bathroom in an orderly fashion. I purchased a travel organizer with pockets that hangs from the bathroom doorknob. I keep all my toiletries and sundries in there. Once ministry time begins, you'll have little control of your schedule. Therefore, it's best to get organized right after you check-in.

You'll also want to find the exercise room or a safe place to walk near the hotel as soon as you check-in. As mentioned earlier, to stay healthy it's important to make diet and exercise a priority. Some ministers establish an exercise regimen they can complete right in their hotel room. Either way, it's critical to intentionally incorporate exercise into your trip.

But the most important item on your organization agenda when you first check in is to plan your daily devotions. Where and when will you sit at the feet of Jesus? Because traveling ministers continually move from place to place, and there is very little downtime, the temptation to neglect their devotional lives will be ever present. Satan will make sure of it. The enemy will whisper in your ear, "Turn on the television and relax," or, "Just pray when you get home."

But neglecting your hidden life with Jesus will generate more problems than you can possibly imagine. For the traveling minister, the spiritual discipline of sitting at the feet of Jesus cannot be skipped. If it is, your Christian walk will begin to decay, and there will be a much greater chance of falling into sin and compromise. (The enemy will convince you that no one will find out.) Therefore find a distraction-free place to seek the Lord. Determine the time of day you'll meet with Him, and stick to it.

AVOIDING ALL APPEARANCES OF EVIL

While it goes without saying that we should stay far away from evil in every form, whether at home or away, there is a particular set of snares that traveling ministry presents. One of the names of the devil is the Accuser of the Brethren (Revelation 12:10 NKJV). The enemy is always looking for opportunities to point his accusatory finger at us, the people of God.

While Satan will falsely accuse us of wrongdoing even when we're innocent, we don't want to hand the opportunity to him on a silver platter.

Therefore, we need to be cognizant of giving even the *appearances* we have committed evil (1 Thessalonians 5:22 KJV). We should err on the side of caution.

The point is this: Never underestimate the nastiness of the devil. He can use one moment with you alone in a room with your male colleague, or a picture on social media with just you and a man, to stir up wagging tongues. (Set your social media settings to require you to approve photos others tag you in).

The enemy can also use a picture of you with a glass in your hand (it's just water but could be misconstrued as alcohol), or even a photograph of you and another woman showing godly affection, to falsely accuse you. (We can never forget that the cultural popularity of ungodly same-gender attraction now requires us to expand our discernment beyond traditional gender boundaries.)

Please hear my heart. I'm not trying to put you into legalistic bondage but ensure you're completely aware of the tactics of the enemy and help you finish your race well. All it takes is a moment of poor judgment to ruin your marriage and your excellent ministry reputation. Having said that, I'd like to introduce to you the "Billy Graham Rule."

The Billy Graham Rule (BGR) is a set of ministry practices that Billy Graham and several other prominent Christian leaders drafted to avoid moral impropriety in their traveling ministries. The premise was to place healthy boundaries around their ministries to eliminate sexual temptation, the appearance of doing something considered morally objectionable, or being falsely accused of sexual harassment or assault. It includes being in the same room alone with, having your picture taken with, and sharing a ride with the opposite sex.

In the seven decades since it was drafted, the BGR has been implemented as a ministry practice by many evangelical leaders. Of recent years it was referred to as the "Mike Pence Rule." Vice President Mike Pence was, however, simply applying the BGR to protect his political career and marriage. Although a vast number of ministers hold fast to the BGR, it also has its dissenters.

There are some who feel the BGR is archaic. The BGR was drafted by all male ministers at a time when female ministerial colleagues were extremely rare. As a woman in ministry, I can attest to the effect the BGR rule has on female ministers. I've been made to feel like a leper in a room of male ministers who treated me as "unclean" by staying as far from me as possible. The BGR can be extremely isolating.

Some critics of the BGR believe the rule is unscriptural. They cite John 4:7-30, the account of Jesus ministering to the Samaritan woman at the well. In New Testament times, Jewish law forbade men from talking to a Gentile woman, especially a woman with a problematic past regarding men. Jesus crossed cultural norms by intentionally approaching and ministering to her. These detractors of the BGR say that a person's soul is eternally more important than adhering to a rule and that diminishing someone's value does not bring them closer to Christ.

Still others believe that the higher our visibility in the body of Christ, the more cautious we must become. They decry that the pastor of a small church isn't as closely scrutinized as someone with a worldwide public platform like Billy Graham. They would say the larger the platform, the stricter the application of the BGR.

My view of the BGR is this: While it's a manmade rule and at times hard to work around and not always achievable, it contains healthy boundaries and is a good goal. Far above the BGR, however, is the leading of the Holy Spirit. Perhaps God would lead some ministers to adhere to stricter standards regarding the opposite sex. For others He may lead them with narrow standards regarding the same gender. Sometimes purity can mean taking extreme measures.

But when the Lord leads me to minister to a man, I obey. However, somewhere in my conversation with him I mention my wonderful husband, and if the conversation takes a turn, and I sense the man is flirtatious, I err on the side of caution and immediately walk away. I also try my very best to not be alone in a room or car, or be photographed with a man. But sometimes it's unavoidable. If it happens, I immediately text my husband. I do the very best I can to avoid all appearances of evil.

RELATIONSHIP BUILDING

The foundation of all traveling ministries should be based on the building of relationships. Far too often itinerant ministers breeze in and out of a church and never make an effort to connect with the pastor after their time of ministry—that is, until they want to preach again or are in need of a donation. This should never happen. It's a form of usury. God is a God of relationships, and He desires for us to enter mutually edifying relationships with one another.

Your ministry relationship starts the first time you preach at the church. You are there to minister to the pastor just as much as you are to the congregation. As a matter of fact, your ministry to the pastor will spill over to his or her congregation. A spiritually healthy pastor can lead to a spiritually healthy church.

Many pastors are (1) fighting discouragement and loneliness and don't have anyone else to talk to, (2) going through an intense trial, wilderness battle, or warfare in their church or family, and (3) in desperate need of refreshment. You can make the difference in their lives! From a pastor's perspective, a guest speaker not only provides a needed break from his or her normal schedule but also an opportunity to receive from heaven.

Ministry needs to continue, however, between speaking engagements. Here are pastor-relationship-building suggestions to incorporate into your ministry:

- Possess a long-term relationship mindset. Think *years* as opposed to *one event*.
- Learn the names of the pastor's spouse and children. Find opportunities to speak into the pastor's life.
- Find ways to serve pastors beyond Sunday. Text them to see how you can pray for them. Ask what you can do to help their churches or ministries. Call them to just listen and be a sounding board.
- Comment on and share their posts on social media. This is a great way to continue to take interest in their lives.
- Keep notes while you're with them on their prayer requests, points of interest, struggles, and projects they are launching. Once you get home you might forget essential information about their lives.
- Be open to God using you to financially sow into their churches. Trust me, some pastors would be shocked (probably faint) to receive a donation in the mail from a guest speaker.
- If you're ministering in the pastor's region, call to see if you can meet him or her and spouse for coffee or a meal—with the motive being entirely to build relationships, not to talk about your ministry.

- Besides sending a thank-you note after your time of ministry, send a gift perhaps at Christmas or for a birthday, a milestone anniversary, or the wedding of the pastor's child. This signals to pastors that you are genuinely interested in their lives.
- Never, ever speak ill about that pastor with another minister—even if the other pastor does. Don't chime in. Not only is it biblically wrong, it will also serve to damage the relationship.

FAITH FOR FINANCES

Jehovah Jireh is your Provider.
Jehovah Jireh IS YOUR PROVIDER.
JEHOVAH JIREH IS YOUR PROVIDER.

Did I mention that Jehovah Jireh is your Provider?

Your faith for needed finances must solely rest in God. Firmly establish yourself in this biblical principle: *"The Lord is my shepherd; I have all that I need"* (Psalm 23:1). If you don't, you'll ride the "trusting in people, systems, and the economy roller coaster," which will let you down and take you upside down and around and around and around.

When I was a pastor, I invited a missionary to speak at my church because I really admired what he was doing for the Lord. The missionary respectfully declined my invitation with no explanation. But word eventually got back to me about the reason he turned down the invitation. I discovered he only spoke at *mega* churches because they give bigger offerings. I shrugged it off and didn't give it another thought. Then the economy took a downward turn, and that same missionary called me to speak at my church. (By the way, I said, "No.")

The mega-church well had run completely dry. The missionary had a system, worked his system, but his system eventually failed him. Man-made systems always will.

Again, I say, your faith must solely rest in God to fund your ministry. You could speak at a large church and receive a $50 offering but at a smaller church receive a check for $5,000. Guest speakers were always amazed at how generous the church I pastored was compared to its size.

It's God who has called you
and God who will provide.

God has given me a big, global vision. This kind of vision requires a large amount of money. As I believe God and am faithful to generously sow into the Kingdom, He will provide. Period. God pays for what He orders, and He equips whom He calls.

If your trust isn't in God to provide, you'll accept invitations that aren't *God-assignments* just because you need the money. You'll also treat ministry as a business. And when there is an economic recession, you'll make ministry decisions based on a failing economy. Determine from the onset of your ministry that you'll never make ministry decisions based on money but solely on the will of God.

> *No one can serve two masters. For you will hate one and love the other; you will be devoted to one and despise the other. You cannot serve God and be enslaved to money.* (Matthew 6:24)

I advise you to ask God for a financial strategy regarding funding your ministry. Every minister needs to follow the leading of the Holy Spirit regarding,

- Raising up monthly, year-end, and one-time donors.
- Whether to work in a secular job or launch a business to help fund your ministry. (Paul was a tentmaker.)

- How to make financial allowances for seasons when ministry is slow (traditionally summer and winter).
- Whether or not to have a product table at your ministry events (a great way to leave a piece of your ministry behind and solidify your message).
- How to cast the vision for your ministry. (Giving follows vision.)
- Whether or not to have a required honorarium, suggest an honorarium range, or accept a love offering. (Unfortunately, many in the Church operate in a poverty spirit, especially if you work a full-time job or they think your husband is the breadwinner.)
- What system to use to keep stellar ministry financial records.
- How generous God will allow you to be (how much to sow into the Kingdom over and above your tithe).

A SERVANT'S HEART

The entire basis of your traveling ministry needs to be selfless service to the Lord. From the moment you step out of the door of your home until you arrive safely back, you are on a missions trip. And your entire trip is an opportunity to minister the gospel of Jesus Christ.

Look for opportunities to minister to hotel, airline, and restaurant employees. God is sending you into that region for a reason. Perhaps you thought you were going on the ministry trip to preach to a particular congregation, but instead, it was to share the gospel with an Uber driver whose grandmom has been praying for his salvation since he was born. Some of my best soul winning adventures have been while traveling for ministry. God is a multi-tasker.

I have a traveling minister friend who carries a $50 bill in her wallet and asks God who to gift it to on her trip. One time, the Lord highlighted to her a maid in the hotel in which she was staying. My friend walked up to the maid, placed the bill in her hand, and said, "This is from Jesus." The maid began to cry as she shared what an answer to prayer that was. That encounter gave my friend an open door to present the gospel to that hotel employee.

When preaching at a church or other ministry venue, your entire motivation is to see how much you can give, not how much you can get. Always go to serve, not to be served. If you can't, then stay home and renew your mind with God's Word until you can.

When interacting with the people before or after the service, give them your absolute undivided attention. Treat them like royalty. If they tell you something exciting about their ministry or family, celebrate with them. If they share a struggle, weep with them. If they talk too long they probably need someone to talk to. So don't shut them down. Honor everyone, all the time, everywhere.

My best advice is to read the account of Jesus washing His disciples' nasty, filthy feet. That posture of humility needs to make a serious comeback in traveling ministry. No demands, no name dropping, no auditioning—only Christlike humility. Wash the feet of the people whom God puts in front of you. Serve the pastor and the people like you are serving Jesus—because you are.

You are an ambassador of Christ.
Represent Him everywhere you go.

CHAPTER 10

Supernatural Ministry

"I wish I could have an anointing
as powerful as minister so-and-so."

IF WE'RE HONEST, we've all had this thought cross our minds. However, the truth remains . . . *you can.* The power of the Holy Spirit can move mightily through you, regardless of your area of ministry specialization.

When I was a senior pastor I would train members of my church to expect God to display His power through them no matter the ministry in which they served—including the greeter ministry. In "greeter training," I would give practical tips (smile, exhibit friendliness, use breath mints, etc.), but I would also encourage them to expect the healing power of God to flow through them as they shook hands with a visitor.

One Sunday morning, a person who had been attending my church only a few weeks motioned for me to come near. The woman said, "Pastor, my body was healed last Sunday." Thinking she received her healing at the altar, I told her how happy I was for her. But then the woman excitedly continued. "When I walked through the door of the church last week, I felt a zap go through my body as the greeter touched my hand to welcome me! The symptoms disappeared and have been gone for the entire week!"

Sister, I share this healing testimony with you to say this:

If God can move in power and might through a church greeter, He wants to do the same through you. Expect and believe. Whether you have a visible, public ministry and stand before masses of people behind the pulpit with a microphone in your hand or your ministry is much more hidden, God wants to use you to do the supernatural works of Christ—and even greater.

> *I tell you the truth, anyone who believes in me will do the same works I have done, and even greater works, because I am going to be with the Father.* (John 14:12)

When Jesus came into the world in the flesh, the power of heaven touched earth. In turn, since Jesus ascended to heaven His followers have carried the power of the Holy Spirit within them in their ministries. Stephen Olford teaches that God's Spirit poured out on earth is "Christ himself, seen, felt, heard, living, active, moving in and through his body on earth."[19] All authority belongs to Jesus, and He has given it to His Church.

In Matthew chapter ten, Jesus conducted missionary training with the twelve disciples, delegating all authority to them.

> *Jesus called his twelve disciples together and gave them authority to cast out evil spirits and to heal every kind of disease and illness.* (Matthew 10:1)

Jesus even delineated the miracles His disciples would see.

---

19 Stephen Olford, *Heart Cry for Revival* (Memphis: Stephen Olford Ministry Legacy, LLC, 2005),

> *Go and announce to them that the Kingdom of Heaven is near. Heal the sick, raise the dead, cure those with leprosy, and cast out demons. Give as freely as you have received!* (Matthew. 10:7-8)

Jesus is the All-Consuming Fire, and the twelve disciples became brushfires, setting everything they touched ablaze with the power of God. Then in Luke chapter 10, Jesus sent out seventy-two disciples. Going out two-by-two, they turned the world upside down with the gospel and returned with this report: *"Lord, even the demons obey us when we use your name!"* (Luke 10:17b).

And then Jesus effectively delegated His authority to every believer in what is known as the Great Commission.

> *Jesus came and told his disciples, "I have been given all authority in heaven and on earth. Therefore, go and make disciples of all the nations, baptizing them in the name of the Father and the Son and the Holy Spirit. Teach these new disciples to obey all the commands I have given you. And be sure of this: I am with you always, even to the end of the age."* (Matthew 28:18-20)

Here is the Great Commission as found in Mark 16:15-18:

> *And then he told them, "Go into all the world and preach the Good News to everyone. Anyone who believes and is baptized will be saved. But anyone who refuses to believe will be condemned. These miraculous signs will accompany those who believe: They will cast out demons in my name, and they will speak in new languages. They will be able to handle snakes with safety, and if they drink anything poisonous, it won't hurt them. They will be able to place their hands on the sick, and they will be healed."*
> (Mark 16:15-18)

Please don't form your theology of supernatural ministry based on what you've experienced (or haven't experienced) regarding the power of God. That's called experiential theology, and it's very dangerous. That's *cafeteria Christianity*—picking and choosing what to believe based on your experience or that of others. No, our theology should be solely based on the Word of God.

Put another way, just because you haven't seen the train come down the tracks in a while—or even at all—doesn't mean there is no such things as trains! Jesus and His Word remain our plumb line in life. If God says it in His Word, we believe it, and that settles it!

You can clearly understand that operating in the supernatural power of God is not just relegated to the famous evangelist on television, the popular Christian conference speaker, or the renowned Christian author, but to ALL WHO BELIEVE! Sister, that's you!

Supernatural ministry should be a reality in the life of every minister of the gospel, no matter the type of ministry.

KNOWING THE PERSON OF THE HOLY SPIRIT

Woman called of God, the key to supernatural ministry is to stay in unbroken fellowship with the Holy Spirit—learning to be led by Him and to cultivate complete and utter dependence upon Him. That will only take place as you develop deep intimacy with the Holy Spirit.

The Holy Spirit, the third person of the Trinity—God the Holy Spirit—is the most important individual and force on earth, and He is the *key* to the glory of God being manifested in your ministry.

The first step to nurturing a close relationship with the Holy Spirit is to understand His attributes, His personality, and His ways. Isn't that the initial stage of any relationship? I implore you to open your Bible and do an exhaustive study on the Holy Spirit with me.

Our study begins with Jesus.

The disciples finally found their Messiah, the Savior of the world—Jesus. He was the absolute love of their lives. But Jesus dropped a spiritual bomb on them when He told them, "*. . . it is best for you that I go away*" (John 16:7a).

Now, I can only imagine what the disciples must have been thinking, "Best for us? How in the world would we be better off without you? We finally found you!" But then Jesus continued with the rest of the story, *"Because if I don't, the Advocate won't come. If I do go away, then I will send him to you"* (John 16:7b).

The Advocate to whom Jesus was referring is the Holy Spirit. Now let's look further in Scripture to find out more about Him.

The Holy Spirit is God. He is as much God as the Father and the Son. He is the third person of the Trinity (Gen. 1:1: Matt. 3:16-17; Matt. 28:19).

The Father is in Heaven; the Son is in Heaven at the right hand of the Father, and the Holy Spirit is the governor of God's kingdom right here on earth (Matt. 28:19-20; 1 Cor. 3:16-18).

He is the Spirit of the Father and the Son. He is the Spirit of the Godhead (Rom. 8:9).

The Holy Spirit is the presence of God on earth. The presence of God is the distinguishing mark of the people of God (Ex. 33:12-19).

He lives in the body of Christ—the Church. We who are born again, and who are by our very nature frail, weak, flawed, perishable and cracked, like jars of clay, are His temple (John 14:17; 1 Cor. 3:6; 2 Cor. 4:7; Eph. 2:21-22).

His indwelling presence makes the weak strong (Rom. 8:26), makes the unsanctified sanctified (Rom. 15:16), and makes the disobedient obedient (Titus 3:5). Without Him, we can do nothing (John 15:5), but with Him we can do all things (Phil. 4:13).

The Holy Spirit is so powerful that He not only indwells individual believers but also unites us with the body of Christ so completely that, collectively, we are one heart, one mind, one Spirit, and one with another (Acts 4:32; Eph. 4:3-6).

Together, we are the Church, the embodiment of the Holy Spirit (1 Cor. 12:12-26).

Individually, we are His residence, but jointly, we are living stones that form the house of God (1 Peter 2:5).

He is a Spirit (John 4:24), but He is also a person. That doesn't mean He has hands, eyes, ears, and operates in a physical body but means He has a personality. He speaks, thinks, feels, works, and exercises His will. He is different in person from Jesus, yet He ministers to us the life, power, and person of Jesus Christ. He makes Jesus real and continues His work. He points us to Jesus and draws unbelievers to Jesus (John 15:26; John 16:14).

The Holy Spirit speaks. He isn't the silent partner of the Trinity as some suppose. The Bible instructs us to pray without ceasing (1 Thess. 5:17). And if prayer is dialogue between man and God, then the Holy Spirit wants to communicate to us without ceasing.

He speaks to us about things to come (John 16:13; Acts 8:26-29; Acts 21:10-11) and about our sin so we can repent (John 16:8).

He gives us the words to say in witnessing encounters (Luke 21:15), instructs us how to pray (Rom. 8:26), and so much more. The way that Jesus talked with His disciples is the way the Holy Spirit talks with us today.

The Holy Spirit knows the thoughts of God and reveals them to us (1 Cor. 2:11).

The Holy Spirit feels and has emotion. He loves (Rom. 15:30), can be grieved (Isa. 63:10; Eph. 4:30), and experiences joy (Gal. 5:22).

He has a will that always lines up with the Father's will, and He exercises that will (1 Cor. 12:11).

The Holy Spirit moves in power and in might (Gen. 1:1-2; Zech. 4:6).

He is invisible, but we can see the effects of where He has been and what He has done (John 3:5-8).

The Holy Spirit is the power of Almighty God, and therefore, He is the most powerful force this world has ever known (Luke 24:49).

He is more powerful than a supersonic jet, the world's fastest computer, and nuclear weaponry combined. He is so powerful that the Holy Spirit raised Jesus from the dead (Rom. 8:11).

When the Holy Spirit moves, He births physical and spiritual life (Gen. 2:7; Rom. 8:11; Matt. 1:18; John 3:5-6).

We cannot enter the Kingdom of God without Him moving in our lives and giving birth to us spiritually (John 3:5).

He is the catalyst of signs and wonders (Mark 16:20), miracles (1 Cor. 12:10), and healings (1 Cor. 12:9). The way Jesus moved in signs, wonders, miracles, and healings 2,000 years ago is the way the Holy Spirit moves on earth today (Heb. 13:8).

In addition to the Holy Spirit's power to perform signs, wonders, miracles, and healings, He also produces in our lives love, joy, peace, patience, kindness, goodness, faithfulness, gentleness, and self-control (Gal. 5:22-23). And in essence, He himself is the personification of all those things.

He is contrary in every way to that of the flesh (Gal. 5:17), which means He is moral, pure, virtuous, completely devoted to the will of the Father, and vehemently opposed in every way to idolatry, witchcraft, hatred, discord, dissensions, factions, drunkenness, orgies, and other works of the flesh (Gal. 5:19-21).

The Holy Spirit can be quenched (1 Thess. 5:19), resisted (Acts 7:51), blasphemed (Matt. 12:31-32), and lied to (Acts 5:3-4). But the results of doing those things can be cataclysmic.

The Holy Spirit is so powerful that He baptizes us with spiritual fire (Acts 1:5) and equips us with our own supernatural, personal, prayer language (Acts 2:1-21; Acts 8:14-20; Acts 10:44-48; Acts 19:1-7; 1 Cor. 14:18).

When we pray in tongues, our spirit prays directly to God (1 Cor. 14:2), totally bypassing our mind (1 Cor. 14:14). Our Holy Spirit prayer language helps to build our faith and recharge our spiritual battery (Jude 20). It strengthens our inner man (Eph.

3:16) and enables us to pray the purposes, plans, and pursuits of God (1 Cor. 14:2).

The Holy Spirit is a gift to us (Acts 2:38), but He himself is also very much a giver. He is the giver of gifts (Rom. 12:6-8; 1 Cor. 12:7-11, 27-31; Eph. 4:11-13), the giver of fruit (Gal. 5:22-26), the giver of encouragement (Acts 9:31), and the giver of direction (Rom. 8:14; John 16:13; Acts 16:6-7). He is the giver of righteousness, peace and joy (Rom. 14:17-19), comfort (John 14:16), and holy boldness (Acts 4:29-33). And He gives us the inward witness of our salvation, assuring us that we are children of God (Rom. 8:16).

The Holy Spirit is our Helper, Intercessor, Strengthener, Counselor, Advocate, Standby, and Teacher (John 14:26).

His attributes can be compared to that of a dove (Matt. 3:16), fire (Acts 2:3), oil (1 Sam. 16:13), water (John 7:37:39; Isa. 44:3; John 4:14; 1 Cor. 12:13), and wind (John 3:8). In Him is wisdom, revelation (Eph. 1:17), understanding (Isa. 11:2), truth (John 14:17), prophecy (Rev. 19:10), and knowledge (Isa. 11:2).

If that's not enough, He is also our rest (Isa. 63:14).

AND . . .

The Holy Spirit is the anointing (1 John 2:27 NKJV) and the distributor of the anointing (Luke 4:14-22).

The anointing is the Holy Spirit's enabling for natural man to do supernatural things (Ex. 29:4-9; Ex. 30:22-33; 1 Sam. 16:1-13). For instance, the Holy Spirit anointed Samson with unparalleled, supernatural strength (Judg. 15:14-15). And when the Holy Spirit departed from Samson, he was left to his own, weak devices (Judg. 16:20-21).

THE ANOINTING

Sister, you are anointed with the power of God to do the supernatural works of Christ.

The anointing on your life and ministry is God's enablement to allow you to do what He has called you to do.

- There are three categories of anointings. They are,

1. The anointing all believers have who are baptized in the Holy Spirit.
2. The individual anointings for what each of us is called to do.

   These anointings are as specific as our fingerprints and are exclusive to each of us. Even if you and I are both called to do the same thing—for example, to pastor a church—and share commonalities in our anointings, there will also be specific anointings that are unique to each of us.
3. The corporate anointings for what an entire church or ministry is called to accomplish for the Kingdom.

   This, of course, is why the enemy always tries to cause division—to hinder the corporate anointing which operates in its fullness in an atmosphere of unity.

The word *anoint*, in the Greek language, means to pour, rub, or smear oil on someone. God loves using visual aids (water baptism, communion, etc.) to illustrate spiritual principles and to symbolize who He is, what He does, and what He wants to do in our lives. Oil is yet another one of God's visual aids.

Friend, God's hand is on your life. His signature has been written on your ministry. His Spirit has been poured onto you. And you are anointed to do a specific work for Almighty God.

In the Old Testament, when the eighty-seven prophets, priests, and kings were anointed for service, oil was poured over them. It was a symbol that God's presence was placed on them to do specific works for God.

The first time the Bible mentions someone being anointed for service was when Aaron and his sons were ordained priests of Israel (Exodus 29:4-9). That anointing ceremony was so important, and had to be so exact, that God even provided the recipe for the anointing oil—down to the specific proportion of spices.

> *Then the Lord said to Moses, "Collect choice spices—12½ pounds of pure myrrh, 6¼ pounds of fragrant cinnamon, 6½ pounds of fragrant calamus, and 12½ pounds of cassia—as measured by the weight of the sanctuary shekel. Also get one gallon of olive oil. Like a skilled incense maker, blend these ingredients to make a holy anointing oil."* (Exodus 30:22-25)

After Aaron was anointed, two things changed.

1. Aaron was set apart for service to God.
2. Aaron was empowered to do a specific work for God.

Before he was anointed, Aaron was the spokesperson for his brother—stuttering Moses. However, after Aaron was anointed, he was set apart and empowered to stand before the Ark of the Covenant as High Priest and atone for the peoples' sins by the blood of the sacrifice. That was something no one besides he and his lineage were allowed to do. Anyone who tried to do that work without the anointing faced deadly consequences.

Woman of God, there is a supply of the Spirit—called the anointing—to set you apart and enable you to do the work of ministry!

It's important to note that God doesn't anoint someone based on natural ability, background, past, intelligence, education, race, or gender. People judge by outward appearance, but God looks at the heart. God anoints whom He anoints, and He has anointed you.

For example, David was anointed King of Israel when he was a young shepherd (1 Samuel 16:1-13). When the prophet Samuel came to David's house to anoint one of Jesse's sons as king, David was the last son whom Jesse brought before Samuel. Aren't you glad that even if we're the last on people's minds to be of service to God (even perhaps by our own families), God can still anoint us and use us in big ways?

Therefore,

- God could anoint a sixteen-year-old teenage boy to do nursing home ministry even though he is young of age and has never experienced the plights of the elderly.
- God could anoint an eighty-year-old woman to evangelize a motorcycle gang even though she's elderly and has never ridden a motorcycle.
- God could (and did) anoint Paul the Apostle to be apostle to the Gentiles even though he had been a *Pharisee of Pharisees* and was a *Jew of Jews* (the polar opposite of a Gentile).

Sister, God chooses whom He chooses, and He has chosen you! Your past mistakes don't matter to God. Your "qualifications" have no bearing on God's decision. God has hand picked you for a redemptive purpose in His Kingdom.

However, the ultimate example of someone anointed by God is, of course, Jesus Christ. And Jesus' last name is not *Christ*. "Christ" means "the anointed one"—*Jesus the Anointed One.*

> *And you know that God anointed Jesus of Nazareth with the Holy Spirit and with power. Then Jesus went around doing good and healing all who were oppressed by the devil, for God was with him.* (Acts 10:38)

> *"The Spirit of the Lord is upon me, for he has anointed me to bring Good News to the poor. He has sent me to proclaim*

> *that captives will be released, that the blind will see, that the oppressed will be set free, and that the time of the Lord's favor has come."* (Luke 4:18-19)

The above two passages not only indicate that Jesus is anointed but also reveal the purpose of His anointing:

- Do good.
- Heal all who are oppressed by the devil.
- Bring Good News to the poor.
- Proclaim the captives will be released.
- Proclaim the blind will see.
- Proclaim the oppressed will be set free.
- Proclaim that the time of the Lord's favor has come.

Woman of God, you are called to do these same supernatural works of Christ under the anointing of the Holy Spirit. But how do you accurately and effectively flow in the anointing? How can you grow in operating in the anointing? And what hinders the anointing from flowing in your ministry?

HINDRANCES TO THE ANOINTING

It's important to understand that there is a cost to flowing in the anointing. The price you pay to walk in the anointing of God is . . . EVERYTHING. You must surrender everything that's not of God and live holy. Sin and compromise will most definitely hinder your anointing. Here is a good prayer to pray: "Father, burn everything out of me that is not of you!"

God doesn't anoint flesh, therefore you must crucify the flesh, die to self, walk in the Spirit, obey the Word of God, and humble yourself under the mighty hand of God. While not a popular teaching in today's Church culture, even among ministers, separating ourselves from the things of this world is what God requires. Those who walk in the Spirit and crucify their flesh will sustain and increase in their anointing.

Living a self-controlled life in your spirit, soul, and body is also a factor in flowing in the anointing. Eat right, sleep well, and exercise. You'd be surprised how feeling tired or sluggish will hinder the anointing from operating in your life.

When I was a pastor, I never went out on a Saturday night (dinner with my husband, a wedding, an outing with friends, etc.). I turned down many an invitation. I never wanted to drag in to church on Sunday morning because I had given myself to entertainment the night before. Jesus deserves my all.

In the same vein, watch what goes in your eye and ear gates, the entrances to your soul and spirit. Sister, please remember that you can't live like everyone else and operate in the fullness of God's anointing on your ministry. This means you can't listen to the same songs, watch the same television shows, or give ear to the same gossip as everyone else. A lot of what Christians allow in their lives isn't pleasing to Jesus. You, my friend, are called higher. The anointing of God is unspeakably precious and valuable, therefore it must be protected.

And although chapter six goes into this in much more detail, it bears repeating here. You must guard your devotional time with Jesus. Spending time in the Word of God and prayer must be a priority, just like it was for the leaders in the early Church. *"Then we apostles can spend our time in prayer and teaching the Word"* (Acts 6:4). Neglecting your devotional time will cause the anointing to dissipate or disappear altogether. You might not notice it right away, but trust me, others do, and eventually it will become loud and clear.

Yes, being with Jesus—the Anointed One—requires you seeking Him with your whole heart. The anointing flows out of relationship, not formula. Sitting at the feet of Jesus, marinating in His presence, letting the Anointed One's oil drip on you, letting it saturate you, is how you obtain the anointing. It's a process. Wanting more of Jesus is the key to flowing in the anointing. When He ceases to be your first love, it will obviously hinder you from flowing in the anointing of God.

While being *with* Jesus is how you obtain the anointing, being *like* Jesus is one of the ways you keep it. Not having the character of Christ will hinder the anointing from flowing in your ministry. Are you the same person in your home as you are behind the pulpit? Do you treat the wait staff at your local restaurant with the same respect as you do someone you greatly admire? Is there any pride in your life? We should ask ourselves these and many other questions in regard to our Christ-like character, or lack thereof.

Also guard your peace and joy no matter what is happening around you. Losing your peace or joy will disturb your spiritual walk and hinder your ability to flow in the Spirit. Frustration and worry will also disturb your spirit and obstruct your ability to hear the voice of God, which is essential for flowing in the anointing.

Walking in your calling on-again and off-again will also hinder your anointing. This has been my observation: A woman of God begins to walk in her calling, I mean she's really going after it, and then she experiences some type of attack of the enemy. So she lays her calling down for a time until that trial is over. And then she picks it back up, but only until she has another personal problem, when she then lays it down again. And this cycle repeats itself. (Of course men will do the same thing.)

You will protect your anointing if you're faithful to your calling in the bad times as well as in the good times. Stay with what God has called you to do in the rain, sleet, hail, sun, and snow; in the winter, spring, summer, and fall; and through adversities, trials, tribulations, heartaches, and disappointments. Remain constant in your calling, and your anointing will remain constant as well.

FLOWING IN THE ANOINTING

While there aren't "Ten Steps to Ministering in the Anointing," there are things we can do to steward it, cooperate with it, increase in it, and flow in it. Here are some.

- **See yourself as anointed.**

  You are anointed for a very specific assignment from God. Once you know what your purpose is, own it. If you don't see yourself as anointed, you won't protect and guard it. And you won't flow in the anointing.

- **Don't go by your feelings.**

  Some days you may feel anointed, and other days you wake up on the wrong side of the bed and don't feel anointed. Good mood, bad mood, living among the unsaved in Sodom and Gomorrah, Nineveh, Babylon, a communist nation, or in the trials of life . . . you are anointed. Some of my most powerful ministry experiences have taken place when I didn't feel anointed. And at other times, when I felt anointed, nothing seemingly happened.

- **Live in the awareness that you carry the presence of Jesus everywhere you go.**

  The Church is meant to be the on-going presence of God in the world through union with Christ and the power of the Holy Spirit. Woman of God, when you show up, in some mystifying way Jesus shows up too. As a minister of the gospel, you are called to be a visual reminder of Jesus to the people—like a living, breathing, walking, communion table. Ministry is living in that awareness. Sister, practice living in that awareness.

- **Look up.**

  When ministering to someone, place your eyes on Jesus. The anointing isn't released when we see a need but when we see Jesus. As Hebrews 12:2 says, *"We do this by keeping our eyes on Jesus, the champion who initiates and perfects our faith."* Put your attention on Jesus, not on yourself or even the person for whom you are praying. Your faith will soar as you keep your eyes on Him. This is especially true when praying for someone who has a dire situation and needs an immediate miracle. Take a step back from the difficult situation and look up at Jesus. Jesus has never changed.

- **Sensitize yourself to the Spirit of God.**

  The world greatly desensitizes us to the spirit realm, so we must intentionally sensitize ourselves to the things of the Spirit by worshipping, praying in tongues much, following the prompts of the Spirit instead of analyzing the prompts of our minds, praying and fasting, and so forth. The more sensitive you are to the Holy Spirit, the easier it will be to flow in the anointing.

- **Draw near to similar anointings.**

  If your anointing is worship ministry, develop relationships with other anointed worship leaders—especially those who are already at the level where you want to be. The anointing is more caught than taught. Drawing close to people with like anointings must be done with purpose and intention.

- **You must keep your anointing fresh.**

  There is nothing like the smell of rancid oil—UGH! Don't coast on yesterday's anointing. Seeking Jesus yesterday was . . . for yesterday. Pressing into Him today is for today. Spending time with Him tomorrow is for tomorrow.

- **Evangelize the lost.**

  God's heart beats for the lost, and when your heart beats like His, He will mightily anoint you. We can never forget that the power of the Holy Spirit poured out on the Day of Pentecost (Acts 2) was the power to be witnesses. Start presenting the gospel to the lost and watch God's anointing grow in your life.

- **Expect God to use you in the Gifts of the Holy Spirit.**

  Part of operating in the anointing of God is to allow the Holy Spirit to give you the spiritual gifts referenced in 1 Corinthians 12:7-12. The purpose of the gifts is not to show the world how super spiritual we are but to bless others. The Holy Spirit distributes the gifts as He wills, but I'm open to Him using me in all nine gifts, at any given time.

- **Walk in love.**

  You can't have more anointing than you do love. Jesus ministered to the masses out of love and compassion, and we are required to do the same. You grow in your love walk when you are faced with the opportunity to not walk in love. As you choose to walk in love—the *more excellent way* (1 Corinthians 12:31 KJV)—you'll flow in the anointing of God with much greater ease.

- **Follow the Holy Spirit's leading.**

  When He gives you instructions, obey His voice. Whatever He tells you to do, do it. If you prepared a ten-page sermon that took you three weeks to research, prepare, and write, and the Holy Spirit tells you to throw it away and go in another direction, do it. The more you yield to the prompting of the Holy Spirit, the better you'll be able to flow in His anointing on your life.

- **Thirst for the presence of the Holy Spirit.**

  He is close to those who desire Him above all things. Practice the presence of the Holy Spirit as you go about your daily routine. Linger in His presence. Long for His presence. Help others to recognize His presence. The anointing is the presence of God on your life and ministry.

Many ministers aren't willing to fully yield to the power of the Holy Spirit. They want to keep control of their sermons, services, and altar times. Others aren't willing to live the "set apart" life required to walk in the fullness of the anointing. Yet others don't have the patience to cultivate an intimate relationship with the Holy Spirit necessary for a mightily anointed ministry. I know that's not you!

When women called of God walk in the boldness and confidence of their identity in Christ, and when they access the anointing on their lives, the earth will witness a greater manifestation of Jesus' fullness and power.

The days we're living in are growing darker and darker. Never has the need been more desperate for ministers of the gospel to flow in the anointing that God has placed on their lives.

The anointing is the supernatural power of God working through natural people to change lives, break bondages, heal the sick, work miracles, and set the oppressed free. The Holy Spirit wants to display His power through you. Determine today that nothing will stop you from flowing in the anointing of God.

CHAPTER 11

Healing from Ministry Wounds

THERE IS PAIN in the ministry.

While there is absolutely nothing in the entire world that compares to the blessing and joy of ministry (and on this we choose to focus), there are also seasons of intense hurt.

I don't say that to scare you, but to prepare you. If you've been in the ministry for any length of time, you already have first-hand knowledge of it. And if you're new, you mustn't be caught unaware.

Soldiers must know there is a possibility they might become wounded. They also need to know what to do if they are. We are in the army of God. We have an enemy. We are in a war. We go from battle to battle. And I don't want you to become a casualty of war.

Jesus warned us there would be pain. As His followers, we should expect to go through some of the same kinds of hurt as Jesus—rejection, scorn, betrayal, misunderstandings, heartache, persecution, hatred, and false accusations, to name just a few. Kingdom leaders experience next-level pain. Hurt will come through sinners masquerading as saints as well as hurting saints who allow the enemy to use them to wreak havoc.

At times, the pain will seem intolerable. The people you thought would never hurt you *will*. You'll be sorely tempted to throw in the towel as you experience the dark night of the soul. That, however, is never an option for those called by the Lord. The word "quit" must be removed from your vocabulary.

After decades of walking in my calling, I'm well acquainted with ministry pain. I don't say that from a place of victim mentality; it's simply a fact. Some of the deepest wounds I've experienced in my lifetime have happened in the ministry.

But here is another fact: I've hurt people, too. Of course my intention has never been to inflict pain. Nonetheless, I have. I've been both the recipient and cause of pain. So have you. It's vital you remember this, especially when you experience hurt. It's easy to lose sight of the fact that we ourselves have inflicted pain on others. We're imperfect people—weak earthly vessels—who will get hurt and, in turn, hurt others.

The New Testament even speaks of painful situations among Church leaders. Paul opposed and rebuked Peter to his face in front of others (Galatians 2:11-16). And the ministry traveling partners, Paul and Barnabas, had such a sharp disagreement that they parted ways and went in their separate ministry directions (Acts 15:36-41). While the Bible doesn't elaborate on their subsequent feelings or emotions, I imagine those rifts were extremely painful. We tend to see New Testament leaders as super humans. They weren't. They were people like us.

Ministry wounds will either propel you forward or backward. When you get to the other side of the incident, you'll either look more, or less like Jesus. Experiencing pain is one of those watershed moments of life. The difference maker is how you respond. Don't waste your pain! More on this later.

In a moment I will delineate several types of ministry pain. But before I do, it's important to clarify something. In no way am I implying that women in ministry experience more pain than our male counterparts. The devil attacks both genders equally. But while there are many similarities in pain points, there are areas of hurt specific to women in ministry, just as there are areas of hurt exclusive to men.

As for the origins of pain in general, some types of pain are inflicted upon us. Others we impose upon ourselves. Still others occur simply because of the passages of life. It's good to keep these things in mind as we deal with pain. And just as there are multiple types of pain and multiple causes for it, the pain of ministry can manifest itself in a myriad of ways. It's crucial that you recognize the distinguishing marks of woundedness so (1) you'll be able to identify the pain you are feeling, and (2) you won't feel like you're the only one experiencing that pain.

Of course even with years of experience there is a point where I am limited by my own experiences and perceptions. So to get a fuller picture of the types of pain in the ministry, I asked hundreds of women in ministry this question:

"What's the greatest pain you've experienced in ministry?"

I received 147 responses.

To be honest, I was surprised, yet not surprised, by the tidal wave of replies I received. Reading their feedback was healing, affirming, and disturbing all at the same time. However, I'm honored to give voice to the pain they've experienced—not for the sake of throwing a woe-is-me pity party, but so I can better prepare you for what may transpire.

There were six common themes articulated by the women in ministry who responded to my question. Under each theme, listed below, I define that category of pain. I then give ten steps to healing from the wounds of ministry.

The six common categories of ministry pain are:

1. Loneliness

Finding friends to share ministry challenges and victories is a great obstacle for women in ministry. This leads to feeling very alone. One of the 147 women who responded gave the following humorous narrative to illustrate the problem of lack of camaraderie with our male ministry peers.

> The male pastors make no effort to include me in their men-only-eating-bacon breakfasts. I love bacon, too! They will include me if they need a secretary. They also don't invite me to their golf games or gun shooting events either. I love to golf, and I'm a good shot! I have finally started working up enough nerve to invite myself along. I even asked if I could ride in the same car, because I usually get pawned off on the female children's pastor. I'm not thrilled about watching sports together, but I'll pack my foam finger and maybe even give it a manicure to get the point across. I make my own fun out of it!

Loneliness is a real and present danger in the ministry and can have devastating consequences. Isolation leads to desolation. If the enemy can isolate us, he can make our lives and ministries a barren wasteland. Sadly, I have a minister friend who has a standing, monthly appointment with a counselor just for someone to talk to because she has no one else.

I highly encourage every woman in ministry to ask God for godly, female friends and trustworthy confidantes with whom she can share the deep things of her heart. Such friends become your *soul café*. God provides all you need for the ministry, including friendships. Ask Him and then keep your eyes open for when He sends them across your path.

2. **Absence of Mentoring**

Mentors for male ministers are scarce, but for women in ministry, they are *really, really scarce*. I have several wonderful mentors now, but I went without a mentor for decades. During that time, my mentors were the biographies of Maria Woodworth-Etter and Aimee Semple McPherson. And I spent thousands of dollars flying across the country to attend conferences in order to receive encouragement for my calling.

The need for mentors is desperate for women called to ministry.

Every female ministry leader needs a mentor to teach her, inspire her, encourage her, pour into her, and challenge her to walk in the fullness of her calling (especially due to the vast amount of opposition she receives regarding her calling).

A mentor helps us heal when we get wounded and walks beside us as we take new Kingdom territory, stay combat ready, build higher, and dream bigger. In addition, women in ministry need a mentor to help them navigate the intricate ropes of being a woman in ministry (something to which male ministers cannot relate).

Therefore, I've dedicated my life to mentoring women called to ministry so that no other woman has to go through the pain of not having a mentor like I did. It's an honor to mentor women called to ministry in their particular area of ministry specialization and help them blaze trails for the Lord Jesus Christ.

Be sure to visit *TrailblazerMentoring.com*

3. **Betrayal**

There is no pain like the pain of betrayal. From my experience, it's the greatest of ministry hurts. Listen to the pained words of Jesus.

Judas, would you betray the Son of Man with a kiss?

(Luke 22:48)

That was the betrayal of betrayals. But God turned around the ultimate betrayal of Jesus by Judas for good. (The outcome was Jesus' death on the cross, which secured our salvation.) And when you are betrayed He will turn around your pain for good too.

There are two parties involved in a betrayal—the betrayed and the betrayer. The betrayer is always someone close to you, or else it wouldn't be classified as a betrayal. Strangers and acquaintances don't cause betrayal. A betrayer is someone you trust. The closer the relationship, the greater your trust, and therefore the greater your hurt and deeper the wound when that trust is broken. The betrayer could be your protégé, friend, staff member, mentor, or even pastor—someone who is a large part of your life and to whom you've opened your heart.

But as hurtful as the betrayal is, the pain of recovery is far more painful. That's why you must push through the pain to get to the other side. There are six stages to the process of recovery from betrayal.

- Shock and devastation ("I thought I knew you!")
- Obsession (It's all you can think or talk about.)
- Anger (Anger increasingly surfaces as more details are exposed.)
- Grief (Things are never going to be the same.)
- Acceptance (The incident becomes part of your new normal.)

And finally,

- Healing

Satan sends betrayal, a low blow sucker punch, to try to destroy our destinies. It's his attempt to hang a chain of sorrow around our necks so we don't move forward. However, God allows it to make us more like Christ. I've experienced three major ministry betrayals thus far, and I can tell you from first-hand knowledge that if you cling to Jesus tighter than you ever have before, it's a win-win even though it feels like you'll never recover.

Trust me, you will!

4. **Cultural and Gender Biases**

By far the most common ministry pain for women is prejudice for being a woman. Sometimes it's subtle, other times overt, but nonetheless, it's a certainty if you are a woman in ministry. This can take many forms, like rejection, being undervalued, getting discounted for positions, the *Second Chair Syndrome*, the limiting mindset that women can only hold positions ministering to women and children, unequally applied rules, intentional blocks, dishonor, and having to work twice as hard as our male counterparts for half the recognition. And these just scratch the surface.

Many times, women in ministry have great difficulty being considered for positions at the local church level, especially senior leadership positions. Often they are only considered for positions that male ministers don't want. One of the 147 women who responded to my question about ministry pain said this:

> I was placed as a lead pastor of a church that had experienced three church splits in twenty years . . .. It's sad that those are the only opportunities that seem to be given to women . . .. However, I will do whatever God has called me to do.

I, too, was placed in a senior pastor role of a church that had twelve members left and was getting ready to close. When women are placed in such undesirable positions, what too often follows is a general lack of support from those to whom one would look for help—leadership.

Bias can also come into play regarding financial remuneration. I preached at a large Christian event and received a $50 department store gift card as my honorarium. The male minister who spoke at the same event a year earlier received a check for $1,500. Instead of the biblical mindset of, "Regardless of gender, we're going to honor and bless the one who delivers the Word of the Lord," it's oftentimes replaced by something like, "Her husband is probably the breadwinner, so we don't have to pay her as much as we do a man."

How pathetic is that?

Accompanying the pain of being the "wrong gender" is what I've coined *Call Justification Exhaustion*. This is the never-ending need to Scripturally defend the call of God on our lives. It's not only hurtful but also tiresome to have your calling attacked on a regular basis.

It's interesting to note that prejudice and bias don't just emanate from male ministers. Our own gender can be our worst critics. This has been my experience. When jealousies, competition, comparison, and insecurities are a factor, it can make for a less-than-welcoming ministry environment. Women in ministry need to learn to be each other's biggest support system.

5. Ministry Transition

Our lives are lived in seasons, and there is a reason for every season. Ministry transition transpires when one season is ending and another one is about to begin. It's that space of time between two ministry assignments.

I picture ministry transition like a long hallway between two connecting rooms. The hallway is plain and has nothing to illustrate the way forward except for a directional sign that says, "Straight Ahead." Although walking through the hallway of transition is exciting, it can also be painful. But you must keep walking toward the open door at the end of the hallway to enter into a whole new dimension of what God has for you.

Transition is painful because it begins with death—goodbyes, leaving your comfort zone, shaking off old ways of thinking and identities, shedding the old wineskin—before stepping into the new dimension.

For the Christian, death always leads to life, yet the grief of death is very real.

If you've given birth, you understand that the stage of labor right before the baby is delivered is called *transition*. This is the most painful part of labor and the time when many women want to give up. However, if she holds on and keeps pushing through birthing *transition*, the birth process will lead to a sudden and priceless revelation of new life. It's the same with ministry transition.

6. **Soldiering On**

Showing up and continuing to push ahead when there's been personal or ministry hurts is another type of woundedness. This is pain within pain. Often there is no time to heal, grieve, or recover from trauma of any kind because ministers must continue putting one foot in front of the other and attend to the needs of others before our own needs. While caring for others above ourselves is part of our calling, at some point we must get well, heal, and rest. And there is often no time, resources, support, or help available for that.

With tears streaming down one side of our faces and a forced smile on the other, we soldier on as we deal with crises in our families, our own personal struggles, naysayers, critics, arm-chair quarterbacks, wolves and witches sent by the enemy, seasons of fruitless feelings when we've sown much but reaped little, grief from burying church members, financial lack, hurts when people we have poured into leave the church, the fishbowl effect (our own distorted views as we try to make sense of things), and disappointments and discouragements of all kinds and at every turn.

In addition, we battle the "But you seem so strong" syndrome. The people around us see the strength of our leadership (because we are operating in Jesus' strength and anointing) and think we don't need help or encouragement. That of course is not true since the pain of soldiering on with our needs not attended to is dangerous for both us and the body of Christ.

Enough about identifying pain, now for your *healing*.

The good news is that no matter the ministry pain, Jesus *the Healer* came to heal the brokenhearted. He made your heart and knows exactly how to put it back together again. In addition, there isn't a ministry pain in which Jesus is not well acquainted. And in each instance of dealing with that pain He models for us the correct response.

While everyone's healing journey is different, and there are no do-this-and-you-will-be-healed formulas for the healing of your broken heart, the following is a list of ten steps I've taken when I've experienced ministry hurt to place myself on the road to recovery.

STEPS TO HEALING FROM THE WOUNDS OF MINISTRY

1. **Get honest with God.**

Lay your heart on God's altar and pour it out to Him—*all of it*. Recount for Him the incident that took place. Share with God the intensity of the pain you are feeling, your questions, and even your anger. Empty your heart out to God. His shoulders are broad. He can take it. Get brutally honest with God. Bring the contents of your heart into the Light of Christ Jesus.

2. **Ask God to perform spiritual heart surgery.**

Our loving Heavenly Father wants to reach His healing hand into your spiritual heart to heal wounds and apply the *Balm of Gilead* to your throbbing heart. Grant Him permission to do just that. Give Him full access to your heart to do what only God can do. In my experience, when I've immediately gone to God to heal my heart, it shortened the duration of the painful trial. When I haven't, it lengthened it.

3. **Surrender your pain to Jesus.**

Picture yourself walking up to the throne of Jesus and saying, "Lord, I give you this pain." And then picture yourself placing it in His hands and leaving it there. If you don't relinquish your hurt, you'll wind up building a memorial to that traumatic event, pitching a tent at its base, camping out, and not moving forward (which of course is what the enemy wants).

Pain can be a distraction. Therefore give your hurts and disappointments to God and leave them there. God longs to turn your battle scars into beauty marks so you'll reflect the image of our Savior.

4. **Extend forgiveness—immediately.**

If you walked into a convenience store to buy a loaf of bread and the price tag read $1,000, would you buy it? Of course not. You would say, "That costs way too much!" Unforgiveness comes with an enormous price tag. It will weigh you down with a heavy emotional burden that you were never intended to carry. Unforgiveness will chain you to that person and incident, and you'll carry them everywhere you go. *Exhausting!*

But here is the highest price of all: If you don't forgive, you won't be forgiven. Forgiveness isn't a process; it's a command. Therefore, out of obedience to God, make a quality decision—from which there's no turning back—to forgive whoever of whatever (*right now!*).

5. **Understand there is more than one victim.**

Yes, you've been the victim of painful words, actions, or betrayal, but the person who hurt you is also a victim. (Don't take on the identity of a victim but that of a victor). In the example of a betrayal, some outside influence penetrated a person's mind and emotions, causing his or her thinking to become skewed and view you as an enemy. While you've done many good things for that person, your betrayer can't recollect any of them—only your deficits. It's like he or she is wearing the dark glasses of deception.

I've found that when offense takes root in someone's heart, it's an open door for Satan to plant a seed that will eventually grow into betrayal. Satan then becomes a puppeteer, and the person who hurt you becomes his marionette. Seeing your betrayer as another victim will help turn your anger into compassion.

6. **Immerse yourself in the Father's love.**

In any painful season of your life, I highly recommend that you meditate on Scriptures that speak of God's love for you and listen to worship music where the lyrics major on the love of God. There is healing in God's perfect, never-ending, unconditional love. Ask God for a fresh revelation of His love for you. Let Him wrap His loving arms around you, hold you with His nail-pierced hands, and pour His love upon you like honey. Oh how He loves you!

7. **Walk in the love of Christ.**

Jesus commanded us to love our enemies. He said even unsaved people can love those who love them back; that's easy. But what He requires from His followers is that we love our enemies (Luke 6:32-36).

Decide from the onset of the incident that caused you pain that you'll be a dispenser of God's mercy. Therefore, when I bump into someone from the past who has caused me pain, I'm the first to approach him or her and express kindness and love. And if someone speaks negatively about that person in my presence, I stop them. Step #6 above will enable you to do this step.

8. **Pray for him or her.**

In addition to walking in love toward a person who hurts us, Jesus also tells us to pray for him or her (Matthew 5:44). But practically speaking, how is that done? I pray for my enemies using the fruit of the Spirit found in Galatians.

But the Holy Spirit produces this kind of fruit in our lives: love, joy, peace, patience, kindness, goodness, faithfulness, gentleness, and self-control. There is no law against these things!
(Galatians 5:22-23)

I pray, "Lord I ask you to encounter her with your *love*. Fill her with your *joy*. Engulf her with your *peace*."

I also use the fruit-of-the-Spirit prayer model every time something triggers me to think about the painful incident that transpired with all of its associated negative emotions. When that happens, through prayer I release the fruit of the Spirit into that person's life. And as I do, the toxic emotions and darkness in my mind lift.

Light chases darkness.

9. **Recalibrate your faith.**

When we're sucker punched by the enemy, it's like we've experienced our own spiritual Pearl Harbor. This can deal a blow to our faith and blur our vision for the future. If we aren't careful, our expectations of the future can reflect the hardship through which we've just gone.

Ask God to recalibrate your faith to echo what God said to Jeremiah.

> *"For I know the plans I have for you," says the* LORD. *"They are plans for good and not for disaster, to give you a future and a hope."* (Jeremiah 29:11)

And dust off your ministry mission statement. Ask God to help you to continue to run the race of your calling with reckless abandon.

10. **Look more like Jesus.**

Ministry pain acts as a sifter. It not only sifts ill-intentioned people out of our lives but also helps to crucify our flesh like nothing else. Often a sifting will occur before God is getting ready to do something BIG in our lives.

One time I was recounting to another minister a painful incident that had just transpired, and he responded, "Congratulations, God is getting ready to promote you! There are things from this season you can't take into the new."

For my doctoral dissertation I interviewed twenty-two pastors who had experienced a major outpouring of the Holy Spirit in their churches. Every one of them told me that an extremely painful incident had taken place in their lives immediately before revival broke out. Each incident was very different but nonetheless excruciating. One of them said, "There were things God needed to do in me in order for Him to trust me with His glory."

There is purpose in the pain. Ask God to use the painful incident with which the enemy meant to destroy you to make you more like Jesus. Isn't that, after all, our ultimate goal—to look more like Jesus? To help you do that, I highly recommend a book by Gene Edwards, titled, *Crucified by Christians*. It's a must read for every Kingdom leader!

Now let me pray for you.

> Dear Heavenly Father,
>
> I lift up before you my sister, whose heart has been wounded by a ministry pain. I ask you to comfort her by your Holy Spirit. Reach your healing hand into her heart and close any open wounds. Help her to release and forgive everyone who has hurt her. Speak to her whatever she needs to hear to see the entire incident from your perspective and to ascend above the pain into your purposes for her life. Help her to walk in love and pray for the person who hurt her. And use the entire hurtful situation to make her more like Jesus. Lord, work your amazing goodness in her life and create a powerful testimony from all that has transpired.
>
> In Jesus' name. Amen!

CHAPTER 12

Wisdom for Staying the Course

I have decided to follow Jesus;
I have decided to follow Jesus;
I have decided to follow Jesus;
No turning back, no turning back.

THE LYRICS OF this old hymn should be the anthem of every minister of the gospel. The day we became born again we gave God our *YES*. And when we received the call to ministry we again gave God our *YES*. We continually give God our *YES* no matter the difficulty or turn of events. Woman of God, there is no turning back.

"Lord, I ask you to take this messed up girl, and if you can do anything with her life, I ask you to do it. I will go wherever you ask me to go, do whatever you ask me to do, and say whatever you ask me to say. I am yours."

That was my prayer when I became a follower of Christ thirty-three years ago. Although I was a brand-new believer and didn't realize all God would ask me to accomplish for Him, I meant every word. Ten years later, I received my calling to the ministry.

That particular morning, as I sat in our recliner conducting my usual morning devotions, the Lord's presence flooded our living room.

God proclaimed, "You have been called and chosen to evangelize the nations."

I was overjoyed and shocked all at the same time.

A plethora of questions flooded my mind: "How do I start?" "Where will I get the needed finances?" "When is it going to happen?" "Where will He send me?"

I rejoiced that God had officially called me. Undaunted by my unanswered questions and entirely devoted to following Him, I was fully prepared to do anything He required.

And I always will be.

Sadly, however, statistics reveal that 42% of ministers at some point in their tenure consider leaving the ministry (Barna.com). Many pastors are only hanging by a thread; it wouldn't take much for them to walk away. The reasons for that are many and varied, but include,

- Discouragement.
- Disillusionment.
- Immense Stress.
- Burnout.
- Lack of financial support.
- Feeling underappreciated and disrespected.
- Feeling used and abused.

- Frustration.
- The toll it takes on his or her family.
- Conflict fatigue.
- Feeling lonely and isolated.
- National upheaval and division that affects the Church.

While all these negative occurrences and more can transpire during your ministry, it's crucial you take the word *quit* out of your vocabulary.

This is one of the healthy boundaries I've placed around my life and ministry: No matter how hard or demanding, I will be a minister of the Lord until the day I graduate to heaven. I made the decision years ago that quitting is not an option.

Sister, if you don't quit, you win!

YOUR PAIN THRESHOLD

See, here's the thing, every minister of the gospel has a pain threshold.

Our threshold of pain defines the limit to how much we're willing to push through the trials of life and ministry. It determines how long we'll continue steadfast in times of difficulty. Our pain threshold is the level of pain we're willing to tolerate when the hordes of hell are breathing down our necks and their claws are in our backs.

A low pain threshold will affect the longevity of any ministry. Even if we experience a level of success in ministry, a low pain threshold affects the length of time it will be sustained. At some point, we won't continue if we don't cultivate perseverance.

But even if we don't leave the ministry, we can give up inside. I've witnessed many ministers possess an inner resignation. While it appears that they're staying the course of ministry, they're no longer advancing the Kingdom. They're maintaining status quo—just enough to keep the ship afloat.

A low pain threshold places a cap on how God can use us. It will stymie our passion for God. But a high pain threshold takes all limits off our pursuit of God.

But pushing through the pain isn't just forging ahead, bearing under, or putting up with opposition of every kind. It's also about the attitude we have while we persevere. James gave us a key to this.

> *Dear brothers and sisters, when troubles of any kind come your way, consider it an opportunity for great joy. For you know that when your faith is tested, your endurance has a chance to grow. So let it grow, for when your endurance is fully developed, you will be perfect and complete, needing nothing.* (James 1:2-4)

When James penned his epistle, Christians were experiencing intense persecution—the kind of persecution to which most of us cannot relate. He admonished them to persevere no matter how difficult their circumstances. Regardless of the pressure, stress, or ordeal, they were admonished to stand their ground with unflinching faith and joy. Faith, coupled with persistence and bolstered by joy, is everything minsters need to have victory in adversity.

Every unfavorable ministry situation presents an opportunity to increase our threshold of pain. But how do we do that? When everything in us screams to not persevere, but we persevere anyway, we raise our threshold of pain.

Every negative circumstance that ministry presents is an opportunity for us to say, "I quit!" But instead, because we've learned how to endure, our pain threshold is raised. Woman of God, there is purpose in the pain of perseverance.

Again, God doesn't waste pain!

Jesus is worth any amount of pain you must endure to be everything for Him. No cost is too great in your hot pursuit of Jesus.

CONSTRUCTING HEALTHY BOUNDARIES

It's also of the utmost importance to place healthy boundaries around your life and ministry. Those boundaries act as a fence that has been erected around the limits of your property. They protect our God-given assignments and responsibilities, help us keep our priorities in order, and safeguard all that has been entrusted to us.

If you're married, your wedding band is another example of a physical boundary. This ring is your announcement to the world that you've entered into a covenant of marriage with your husband in the presence of God. Your wedding band helps keep your marriage healthy. It sends a clear message to potential suitors, flirters, and adulterers: STAY AWAY. I'M TAKEN.

God defines our lives and ministries, and then we create healthy boundaries to protect our callings, families, marriages, personal convictions, core values, and hearts. Boundaries keep all the good things in and all the bad things out.

Godly boundaries will protect your God-given purpose, help you live a disciplined Christian life, eliminate distractions, and stay focused. They will help you effectively manage time, avoid getting overwhelmed, and dodge burnout. Healthy boundaries will make you a better steward and help you keep the main thing the main thing.

Out of His love for us, God has given us boundaries through His Word. The Bible contains healthy boundaries in the form of commandments, biblical precepts and principles, wisdom, direction, and instruction. One example is the Sabbath Day rest.

True confession: For the first eight years of my pastorate, I worked seven days a week. I never took a day off in all those years. I'm goal-oriented, strategic, and driven. Many describe me as intense. But I describe myself as passionate.

I worked with intensity and passion to evangelize the nations, call the Church back to prayer, contend for revival, and mentor others to set the world on fire for Jesus Christ. I didn't have time for a day off.

One day the Lord strongly convicted me—no, *rebuked me*—of violating His Word and my need to repent for not taking a weekly day of rest. In hindsight, the results of working every day straight for eight years were starting to show up in my ministry and in my life. I made a gargantuan course correction.

Now I take off every Monday. Other Kingdom leaders take their Sabbath Day rest on Friday or Saturday. Woman of God, choose a day of rest and guard it like the Hope Diamond. Make it a boundary. Don't check your ministry email, text messages, or voice mails. Trust me when I say there will always be people who try to cross this boundary. I've received many a phone call or text message that starts like this: "Pastor, I know it's your day off, but . . .."

One time, I foolishly answered one of those text messages on my day off. The person had texted to tell me her sister needed urgent prayer. I thought, "I better respond to this important text. Maybe her sister was in a car accident or something even worse." I texted her back, "How can I pray for your sister?" She responded: "My sister is in pain because she just stubbed her little toe!"

Lesson learned the hard way! I never made that mistake again.

In this same vein, another healthy ministry boundary is to establish a regular work schedule—*and then stick to it*. Why? The work of ministry is endless. Solve one problem, there will be another one. Put out one fire, there will be another fire right around the corner. Counsel one person, yet another hurting person is waiting in the wings.

While there are emergencies that inevitably will interrupt your time management plan, you need to have an established work schedule that you generally stick to and make widely known.

A plan for self-care is yet another healthy boundary you should incorporate into your life. Admittedly, I don't like the word *self-care*. It sounds . . . well . . . selfish. So for years I resisted the idea and didn't take care of my temple as I should. Unfortunately, I eventually paid the price. If you don't take care of yourself, your ministry will surely suffer. Make it a priority to keep yourself well (diet, exercise, fun, etc.). If *you* don't, trust me, no one else will.

Sister, take time alone with the Lord to establish Spirit-led, healthy boundaries to protect your life and ministry. Review them often. Make them known far and wide. Determine to abide by them whether or not people like it, understand it, or try to challenge it. You perform for an audience of one: God. If He is pleased with you, that's all that matters.

The voice of Almighty God is what you obey. None other.

KEEP YOUR JOY TANK FILLED

Joy is no small thing.

We have a tendency to minimize joy like it's no big deal if it's missing. But joy isn't optional or non-essential to our Christian walk or ministry. It acts as a barometer of our spiritual strength, because "*. . . the joy of the LORD is your strength*" (Nehemiah 8:10).

Much joy equals much strength. Little joy equals little strength. Friend, I repeat, joy is no small thing, especially as it pertains to ministry. Kingdom leaders are strong in the Lord because they have fullness of joy. In stark contrast, when ministers lose their joy, like an automobile's check-engine light, that loss signals something is very amiss.

My first car was a boxy, cocoa-brown 1976 Ford Granada (aka The Lemon). The beige interior smelled like mildew and the *Armor*

All that I used to cover up the musty smell. My mom purchased the car from her co-worker two weeks before my driver's test so it would be ready and waiting when the big day arrived.

With my new driver's license in tow and a grin from ear to ear, I headed down the road to start my new life of independence . . . for about a mile. The Lemon quickly overheated. The car apparently had an oil leak. The dipstick was bone dry. My badge of newfound freedom turned into a crash course on teenage auto mechanics.

What oil is to a car, joy is to our relationship with God. A dry oil tank will cause a car engine to burn up. But a joyless ministry life is infinitely more dangerous. Without joy, we'll burnout, wear-out, or give-out. We need to pay close attention to our joy levels.

Joy isn't a feeling, and it isn't the same as happiness. Feelings are fleeting and fickle, and happiness is a feeling that originates in the mind.

Happiness is encrusted with external and temporary adornments. Joy and happiness are completely different.

Joy is of the heart, and it's a byproduct of the pursuit of Christ. It's a fruit of the Spirit (Galatians 5:22-23). And it originates from the throne of God. Joy comes giftwrapped in contentment, beauty, and trust. It can bloom right next to grief, loneliness, or disappointment and starve whatever negative emotions are nearby.

We can't lather up joy. Having it is a choice. Our joy grows when we have the opportunity to not be joyous but continue in joy in spite of it. Joy diminishes when we're enticed to cast our joy aside and give temptation sway.

Here's something startling. The spiritual maturity of a Christian leader can be measured by what it takes to steal her joy. *Ow!* A minister of any maturity level can experience joy right smack dab in the middle of a miracle. Who can't do that? But the spiritually mature leader also lives with joy between miracles. Between the miracles is where authentic ministry is lived.

To fix The Lemon's oil leak, I had to find where the oil was leaking. It's the same with joy. We can find ourselves joyless but completely unaware how we arrived at that condition. That's why it's important to recognize "joy leaks."

I've experienced "joy leaks" when,

- I had my eyes on the circumstances of ministry.
- I stopped being eternity-minded.
- I put ministry to others before ministry to God.
- I ceased doing everything unto the Lord, and my motive became anything else.
- I chose discouragement in lieu of joy.
- I allowed fear, doubt, or unbelief in my heart. (Faith and joy are partners.)
- I stopped walking in my purpose.
- I had unrepented sin in my heart.
- I focused on self instead of others.
- I wasn't casting all my ministry cares upon the Lord.

Do you recognize any of these "joy leaks" in your life or ministry? If so, run to the foot of the cross. Stop the joy from draining out by repenting, and ask God to restore the joy of your salvation.

Sister, protect your joy though the hordes of hell attack from every angle. Joy responds to every matter of life from a heavenly perspective. As a matter of fact, when we walk in the joy of the Lord we get a foretaste of heaven.

When miracles delay, your joy will stay.

Jesus is your joy.

LOVE GOD, LOVE YOUR NEIGHBOR

It's of the utmost importance, woman of God, that you guard your love walk—your love walk with both the Lord and His people. As Luke 10:27 states, *"You must love the Lord . . ."* and *"Love your neighbor . . . ."* This remains the sum of our Christian walk. Therefore, it must be the priority of our ministries.

The first thing we must do to guard our love walks is to ensure our love for Jesus never shrinks but is ever growing.

Nothing should ever take Jesus' place in our lives. Jesus should take precedence over everything. But, sadly, the busyness, pain, and long hours of ministry can easily diminish our first love.

To illustrate, imagine for a moment a woman standing in a room listening to rousing music. Her foot taps to the beat. Her torso sways. And she breaks out in dance. It's apparent to everyone watching that she thoroughly enjoys the music.

Next, a deaf woman enters the room. She observes the delight of the first woman and desires the same experience. So the deaf woman mimics the first woman's every move. In the beginning, she remains awkward and clumsy, but with practice she begins to mirror the first woman's actions.

At first, there seems to be little distinction between the two dancing women. But on closer examination, a huge disparity exists. The first woman is responding to the beautiful music, while the deaf woman is merely imitating the first woman.

I think I know the deaf woman. *She's me.*

Unfortunately, there have been seasons of my Christian walk when I've caught myself going through the spiritual motions.

While on the surface an onlooker would never have been able to tell since I still spoke *Christianese*, checked off my devotional boxes, and worked hard at being a good *Martha* for Jesus, somewhere along the way I'd lost my first love—just like the church in Ephesus.

Chapter two through three of Revelation presents five churches in desperate need of revival, including the church in Ephesus. In Revelation, we read that John was told to write to the five churches, and he was told what to say to each of them. In his message to the church in Ephesus, they received a severe rebuke from the Lord, who warned them of dire consequences if they didn't repent.

The Ephesian Christians had lost their first love (Revelation 2:1-7). Though they vivaciously danced for the cause of Christ, they had stopped hearing the music.

Their love for Jesus had dissipated.

Rewind several decades earlier. We read in Acts chapter nineteen that the church in Ephesus was in the throes of revival. The gospel was preached. Multitudes were saved. And missionaries were sent forth. In addition, churches were planted, miracles were performed, and hearts were gripped by the fear of the Lord.

The Ephesian believers had repented of their sins, even to the point of burning expensive magic arts paraphernalia in a common bonfire. To show their love for Jesus, no price was too great. They were passionately in love with Jesus and utterly sold out to Him. What a picture of Christians in revival! (Acts 19:17-20).

The Ephesians started out like the first dancing woman (Acts 19). However, over time they lost their first love and shifted into form (Revelation 2). The fact that it could happen to the church in Ephesus should be a *danger ahead* sign to all of us.

And here's the strange thing. If Jesus drops from greatest-love status, He doesn't hold second place. He plummets to number 435 on our agape scale. If Jesus isn't our top priority, He falls straight to the bottom. Crazy, but true.

Jesus is either our first love or He's not. There's literally no in-between.

So how in the world does this happen? I mean, how does a Kingdom leader go from "No price is too great to show my love for Jesus" to "My love for Jesus has died a lukewarm death"?

The obvious answers are sin, compromise, worldliness, not guarding your eye and ear gates, and so forth. However, I've found that it's the not-so-recognizable *love extinguishers* that have been the biggest detriment to my love for Jesus.

Following are ten "first love" questions that have helped me rekindle my love for Jesus. Prayerfully use them to examine your heart.

1. Have I become so familiar with Jesus that I've taken for granted His redemptive work on the cross?
2. Have I become apathetic in any way toward my relationship with God?
3. Have I let ministry distract, crowd out, or diminish my love for Jesus?
4. Have I reduced my quiet time with Jesus to a timeslot in my bloated ministry schedule?
5. Have I let the cares of ministry cause my passion for Jesus to become dull?
6. Have I let hardness of heart creep in due to ministry pain?
7. Have I shifted my focus from loving Jesus to working for Jesus?
8. Have I lost my simple devotion to Jesus by complicating my Christian walk?

9. Have I become so battle weary that I no longer enjoy my relationship with Jesus?
10. Have I lost the wonder I had for Jesus when I first became born again?

I don't know about you, but these questions really trouble me. I hope they always do.

Is the Holy Spirit convicting you today? He is me! *Run* into the arms of our merciful God and fall in love with Him all over again. Ask Him to awaken the passion that was once ablaze in your heart.

After dealing with the first priority of loving God, the second thing we must do to protect our love walks is to love God's people like we do ourselves.

We need to love others with the measure that we care, protect, and love our own lives. However, sometimes that's hard to do. The people in our churches or ministries can at times be difficult to love. Sometimes they are just as hard to love as we ourselves are hard to love. (I know this is tough to believe!)

People can be unreasonable. Love them anyway. They can be selfish. Love them anyway. Tomorrow they will forget what you did for them today. Love them anyway. People can tear down overnight what you spent years building. Love them anyway. People who say they need help will attack you as you're helping them. Love them anyway. For some people, your all is never good enough. Love them anyway.

I've found one of the main keys to loving the unlovable is to be quick to forgive when people hurt you. If unforgiveness is allowed to remain, it will turn into bitterness. Bitterness poisons love.

When I was new in the ministry, one of my mentors said, "What I'm about to tell you is the secret to success in ministry." I thought he was going to tell me how to raise the dead, receive the mantle of Elijah, or see limbs grow back in answer to the prayer of healing!

Instead, he said, "If you don't get bitter, you'll make it."

I thought to myself, "If you don't get bitter you'll make it? That's the secret to success in ministry?" I was disappointed. But he went on.

"In the ministry, you'll have plenty of opportunities to get bitter. Over the years I've seen many ministers fall from grace and lose their ministries. Many times it began with bitterness of soul. Ministry pain will either make you bitter or better. Choose better. Be quick to forgive, and walk in love."

Now that I've been in the ministry for decades, I realize he gave me the best piece of ministry advice I could have ever received.

Friend, when people cause you pain, forgive them instantly, love them anyway, and never let bitterness encroach upon your heart.

THE SECRET SAUCE—PERSONAL RETREATS

The ministry can be exhausting. I've been to the point of exhaustion on many occasions. How can it *not* be exhausting? In this fast-paced, noisy world in which we live, exhaustion is truly hard to escape.

There have been times I've felt like I was being swept over Niagara Falls in a barrel, unable to tell which end was up. Have you ever felt like that? Which one of us goes through life or ministry unscathed?

Consider human-like-us Elijah. In 1 Kings chapter eighteen through nineteen, mighty Elijah possessed the spiritual strength to confront the prophets of Baal on Mount Carmel (with their legions of demons). And he had the God-given ability to run faster than a horse.

But just like that, this same (mighty?) Elijah fled in fear from Jezebel, sat down under a broom tree, and prayed he would die because it all got to be too much.

However, God supernaturally strengthened Elijah, and He wants to do the same for you! God *will* (notice I didn't say *may* or *can*) give you a second wind as you spend time with Him. He *will* breathe His breath into your life to impart strength and hope. God *will* restore you!

Although trying events in your life may be safely in your rearview mirror (or maybe you are facing them right now), their effects may still linger. To avoid being overcome by depression like Elijah, or to gain a victory over an opposing force—physical or spiritual—we need to intentionally position ourselves to receive God's powerful strength.

While our daily time with the Lord is indispensable to our spiritual well-being (nothing replaces it), I've found this to be true as well:

> Recovery from a protracted battle often calls for protracted time set apart with God.

Take center stage—*drum roll*—the personal retreat. My secret sauce for success and longevity in ministry is taking periodic, planned, personal retreats.

On a personal retreat, you make time and space to give God your full attention and spend unhurried time in His presence. You reflect, refuel, and refocus. You pursue God for . . . well . . . God. You lay your heart on His altar, renew your love affair with Him, and receive oxygen for your soul.

On a retreat, your soul stands alone with God. You unlearn and relearn. God takes out, puts in, and rearranges. Your priorities get reshuffled. (It's amazing how God pinpoints the things that really matter—and those that don't.) God soothes your battered heart and wipes tears from your sorrowful eyes.

In the stillness of a personal retreat, you realize your heart has unhealed wounds and the life of God has drained out of you like the slow leak of a tire. In the quiet of a retreat, these things simply can't go unnoticed.

When you intentionally set yourself apart with God for an extended period of time, your innermost thoughts cascade, and you receive needed assurance of His promises for your life. As you marinate in His presence and stop "doing" for God (He can raise up a donkey to do the same), you are reminded that the greatest yearning of your heart is, "I desire you and you alone."

God will accomplish a myriad of things when you slow down, unplug from the noise, and enjoy precious hiddenness in Him. Some of what He accomplishes during a retreat, you'll be able to articulate; as for others, you won't have the words. But like our friend Elijah, as ministers of the gospel we need to spend time alone with God beneath the broom tree (or house plant) and receive God's presence to renew our strength.

I take a one-day retreat every month, a three-day retreat every quarter, and a seven-day retreat once a year. And this is important: I take them whether I feel I need one or not. But because of the urgency of ministry, there've been times when I skipped a previously scheduled retreat. I told myself, "I'm fine. I can cancel this one time." M-I-S-T-A-K-E! Trust me when I say the results of *not* taking the retreat eventually reared its ugly head.

And I have to emphasize, a retreat is not a vacation! It's also not a family reunion, a tourist get-away, or a girls' weekend. It's you and God—alone—for the sole purpose of seeking Him with your whole heart. That's not to say you can't take a half-day or full-day retreat during your vacation. But it's important not to confuse the two.

"But you don't know my calendar. I can't afford the time to take a personal prayer retreat." To that I say, you can't afford ***not*** to. You may have to juggle or finagle to find time, but it's there—somewhere. You just have to find it. Let me rephrase it like this: If we can find time to binge watch all nine seasons of ___________________, we can find extended time to *be with Jesus.*

Please schedule it. Post haste.

I've taken half-day, full day, 24-hour, three-day, and seven-day retreats. In my experience, if you don't have D-A-Y-S on end for a personal prayer retreat due to circumstances beyond your control, God will honor the time you can dedicate to Him. But if you can steal away for an extended length of time, *do it!*

"Where can I go on a retreat with the Lord?" Let me answer your question with a question.

Where do you best hear from God? Looking over the expanse of your Christian walk, where have you been when you've heard God's voice the clearest?

Our relationships with God are all so different. For me, God's voice is the loudest, and His presence is most tangibly felt, when I'm away from the familiar—literally anywhere, as long as it's unfamiliar. Elijah's place of refueling was a solitary broom tree. Where's yours?

I've taken prayer retreats holed up in a hotel room, a bed and breakfast, and in my church's prayer room (with air mattress in tow). I've also spent prolonged time with God at a friend's home as well as on a park bench staring at a lake (a half-day retreat location). Regardless of where your retreat is conducted—local or distant, expensive or frugal—it will be a sacred space to meet with God.

At the start of my retreat, I anoint myself with oil to consecrate myself to God's purposes during my time with Him. Then I prayerfully determine the type of fast I am undertaking. (Fasting coupled with prayer is spiritual *DYNAMITE!*)

I pack my Bible, notebook and pen, prophetic words I've received over the years, worship music, and communion elements. And I ask God if there are any other Christian books I should take—books through which He wants to minister to me.

I also establish a loose retreat plan. "Loose," because the Holy Spirit orchestrates the retreat and moves as He wills.

To help you get started, here is a sample retreat schedule that has proven highly effective for me:

- Read Bible
- Pray
- Listen
- Journal
- Give thanks
- Worship
- Pray in the Spirit
- Rest

Repeat this rhythm for the duration of the retreat.

Regardless of the retreat length, location, or schedule, accept Jesus' irresistible, personal-to-you invitation.

> *. . . Come to me, all of you who are weary and carry heavy burdens, and I will give you rest. Take my yoke upon you. Let me teach you, because I am humble and gentle at heart, and you will find rest for your souls. For my yoke is easy to bear, and the burden I give you is light.* (Matthew 11:28-30)

Woman of God, schedule your intentional easy-yoke, burden-light retreats with Jesus on your calendar.

Jesus

Is

Your

Rest.

Lord, I can't go on like this. I'm exhausted and discouraged from the battles of ministry.

Please help me. I lay my heart on your altar.

I've reached my pain threshold and violated my healthy boundaries.

Examine my heart, restore my joy, soften my heart, and encounter me with your love.

Under this broom tree, I find refuge for my weary soul.

You provide water to quench my thirst.

You place hot bread before me to impart strength.

I hear your gentle whisper.

You are here.

SELAH

CHAPTER 13

The Indescribable Rewards of Ministry

WOMAN OF GOD, we've covered an abundance of mentoring wisdom. Throughout this book I've endeavored to equip you for the work of ministry by addressing as many topics, challenges, and questions as possible. Although much more could be said, I concentrated on the specific aspects of ministry on which the Lord had me focus.

You learned to identify, prepare, protect, and defend your calling. In addition, you were taught how to prepare messages, navigate the rigors of traveling ministry, and find mentors, protégés, and friends to invite into your life. You were also made ready to minister in the supernatural power of the Holy Spirit, heal from inevitable ministry pain, and stay the course of your calling, no matter the difficulty.

And now we will end with why we do what we do.

Although we live in a world soaked with evil and are constantly swimming against the tide of deceptive ideologies and philosophies, and although the demands of ministry at times seem too heavy of a load, the end *will* justify the means.

Nothing you do for the Lord goes unnoticed by Him. Great eternal rewards await as you are faithful to fulfill your God-given assignment. God rewards those who sincerely seek Him (Hebrews 11:6).

GOD IS A REWARDER

For many years I didn't pay much attention to the rewards spoken of in the Bible. After all, I don't walk in my calling for the reward. To be honest, I'm always surprised when I remember there are rewards. I live in my purpose out of love for Jesus, not for the reward.

But about five years ago I had a change of heart regarding the topic of biblical rewards when I received the following revelation.

> If the Word of God teaches there are rewards, and if the Word defines both the kinds of rewards that exist and the conditions for receiving those rewards, then rewards are important to God. And if they are important to God they need to be important to me.

So I came to the conclusion that *not* caring about rewards is not biblical.

The subject of rewards is one of the most important themes in the Bible. Jesus referenced *rewards* over fifty times. Therefore, the topic is obviously worthy of study. Interestingly, in thirty-three years of walking with the Lord I don't recall hearing one sermon about rewards. So I embarked on an intensive study on rewards.

With my Bible open and concordance in hand, I studied a myriad of verses referencing rewards, including this one:

For the Son of Man is going to come in his Father's glory with his angels, and then he will reward each person according to what they have done. (Matthew 16:27 NIV)

As I meditated further on the words of Matthew sixteen regarding rewards, I understood the following truths through the filter of the Holy Spirit.

- Jesus is coming again.
- He will bring rewards.
- Rewards reflect how we lived while on earth.
- Nothing we do for the Kingdom of God goes unnoticed.
- The rewards we receive will be based on what we've done.
- Salvation is not based on works. But our rewards are.
- We will each have a different measure of rewards.
- Some won't receive rewards.
- God delights in expressing how He feels for all we did for Him.
- Rewards help us remain eternity-minded.
- Rewards comfort us during pain, sacrifice, and persecution.
- Rewards help us shake off apathy, procrastination, and disobedience.
- Rewards remind us that the choices we make have eternal consequences.
- God's character is to reward.
- Rewards are important to God.

Therefore, as stated earlier, rewards are important to me. And I want them to be important to you.

The ultimate reason I penned this book was so you would walk in the fullness of your calling to win a vast harvest of souls. And it's for this that you'll be richly rewarded.

The rewards of the Bible come in distinct forms. The Word of God speaks of rewards as our offspring (Psalm 127:3), as garments in varying degrees of glory (Rev. 3:4-5, 19:1-8), as authority (Matt. 19:28-30, 25:23; Luke 19:17-19, 22:29-30; Rev. 2:26, 3:21), as treasures (Matt. 5:12, 6:4, 10:41-42, 16:27, 19:21), and as the eighteen different rewards listed in Revelation chapters two and three, which contain the seven letters to the seven churches.

But in my closing thoughts to you, I want us to focus on the eternal reward of *crowns*.

THE FIVE CROWNS

Although the Bible doesn't describe their physical appearance, the crowns God places on our heads to reward us for our love, faithfulness, and dedication to Him while on earth will be more glorious than we could ever imagine. As sparkling and magnificent as earthly crowns are that belong to royalty, heavenly crowns will far surpass them because they express the honor, power, dignity, beauty, worth, and glory of Almighty God.

There are five reward crowns spoken of in the New Testament. Each one represents a different heavenly reward with its own set of qualifying conditions. It's important to note that it's possible to lose an eternal crown if we're not steadfast in our love and obedience to God by finishing our race. Jesus said, *"I am coming soon. Hold on to what you have, so that no one will take away your crown"* (Revelation 3:11).

Woman of God, if you fear God and not people, if you please God and not people, and if you obey God and not people, you'll receive a multitude of heavenly rewards. This cannot be emphasized enough, because there will be constant pressure to cave in to the opinions, wills, and plans of people.

In addition to receiving a heavenly reward for living a life worthy of your calling, you also have the awesome privilege to point God's people toward their eternal rewards. Always remember that a leader may take people where they want to go, but a great leader takes people where they ought to be even if they don't necessarily want to go there.

Your job isn't to tickle people's ears with what they want to hear or turn a blind eye to their sin or compromise. It's to prepare them for eternity.

The five crowns spoken of in the New Testament are analogous to the crowns awarded to athletes in Bible times at the conclusion of races for finishing victoriously. Those earthly crowns looked very much like a simple laurel wreath, but they were highly prized.

Although they weren't made of fine metals and precious gems, they were coveted treasures for runners. To them, having the laurel wreath placed upon their heads meant their dedication, perseverance, and commitment to living a disciplined life paid off and they had mastered their sport.

Friend, there could be no greater reward than when Jesus personally places a heavenly crown on your head to reward you for your commitment to fulfilling His plans, purposes, and pursuits for your life. And just think about your fingerprints being on the lives of other believers, either directly or indirectly, when they receive their crowns. No words can express the joy of seeing that!

Here are the five crowns mentioned in the New Testament for Christians who have been faithful to God's call until the end. I pray this is of great encouragement to you.

1. **Crown of Incorruption** (1 Corinthians 9:25)

   Paul described this crown as given to believers who live disciplined lives and refuse to let their flesh impede their marathon of faith.

2. **Crown of Rejoicing** (1 Thessalonians 2:19)

   Also referred to as the Soul Winner's Crown, this crown is given to Christians who fervently win the lost.

3. **Crown of Righteousness** (2 Timothy 4:8)

   Paul described this crown when he was speaking of his own inevitable death. It's given to believers who long for the return of Christ and live holy before the Lord in preparation of His appearing.

4. **Crown of Glory** (1 Peter 5:4)

   Also described as the Pastor's Crown, this crown is given to shepherds and elders who faithfully teach and pastor God's people.

5. **Crown of Life** (Revelation 2:10; James 1:12)

   Also known as the Martyr's Crown, this crown is given to those who stay faithful in spite of suffering persecution, who resist the temptation of the enemy regardless of how difficult, or who physically die for Christ.

Sister, you would do you well to study the five eternal crowns and ask God to cause you to recall what you learned about them whenever the road of ministry seems more than you can bare. Think of them when you wonder if you can continue the good fight of faith.

Anytime you become battle weary, anytime you're in the middle of a fiery attack from the enemy, or anytime you see an arduous path ahead, I encourage you to lift your eyes to Heaven and picture the Lord of lords and King of kings holding your crown in His nail-pierced hands. One day, when you finish your race, He will place that crown on your head.

Again, I want to remind you that God sees all that you do for His people. He remembers and will never forget every act of help, encouragement, kindness, and even correction you bring to the people He dearly loves. He knows you do it out of your love for Him, and He will reward you beyond anything you could ever ask, dream, or imagine.

God sees that you preach the uncompromised Word when many other ministers are yielding to popular opinion. He sees you studying the Bible for fresh Bread from Heaven and a word in due season for the body of Christ. God sees you admonishing His people to live holy lives before Him with clean hands and pure hearts.

He hears you praying big, bold prayers for His people and igniting a thirst for prayer in their hearts. God hears you calling out the names of nations and praying for people across the ocean you'll never meet this side of Heaven.

He hears you in your prayer closet waging war against the enemy on behalf of the people He has entrusted to you. He hears you standing stalwart at the gate of the sheepfold protecting His sheep from ferocious wolves, Jezebels, Absaloms, and even from themselves.

God observes you reminding His people of who He is when they've forgotten. He observes you locking your faith shield with theirs in times of dire need. God observes you teaching His people what it means to love the Lord their God with all their hearts, souls, minds, and strength, and to love their neighbors as themselves. God observes you living an exemplary Christian walk for others to follow.

He watches you obey the Great Commission and teach others to share the gospel and their testimony. God watches as you call out the gifts, talents, and purposes in the lives of His people and thrust them into the harvest field.

He watches you look into the faces of the unsaved with the confident knowledge that Jesus is the answer to their every need. God watches you impart a passion for souls into the hearts of believers.

God takes notice that you care for His people at their highest of highs and their lowest of lows. He notices how you hold the hand of a newborn baby in the morning and by nightfall clasp the hand of someone about to graduate to heaven.

God notices how you walk with His people in their mountain-top seasons of celebration as well as in their valley-seasons of despair—even while you are exhausted from fighting your own personal battles. He never fails to notice how you prefer their interests over your own and tirelessly minister to the people He loves.

And He sees you prepare His people for eternity and the persecution to come and teach them to not love their lives so much that they are afraid to die for Christ (Revelation 12:11). God sees you helping them finish the race and get to the finish line with the victor's trophy in hand. And He sees you preparing believers for Christ's Second Coming and imparting to the body of Christ the urgency of the hour.

Because you've willingly laid your life down for Him and will be faithful to Him until the end, God will reward you with crowns, crowns, and more crowns.

CROWN HIM WITH MANY CROWNS

But here's the thing. Jesus is our ultimate reward. He is our reward here on earth as well as in Heaven. Jesus is the very definition of reward. All rewards, no matter how great, pale in comparison to seeing the face of our Savior.

I want to receive crowns, crowns, and more crowns so I can lay them at the feet of Jesus—the only one worthy to receive glory, honor, and praise. He is my reward. As I gaze at Jesus' beauty, I'll say, "Jesus, you're the only reward I need."

> *Whenever the living beings give glory and honor and thanks to the one sitting on the throne* (the one who lives forever and ever), *the twenty-four elders fall down and worship the one sitting on the throne (the one who lives forever and ever). And they lay their crowns before the throne and say,*
>
> *"You are worthy, O Lord our God,*
> *to receive glory and honor and power.*
> *For you created all things,*
> *and they exist because you created what you pleased."*
>
> (Revelation 4:9-11)

If the Lord chooses to place eternal crowns on my head, I will lay those crowns at Jesus' feet and worship Him.

I will say,

Lord, these crowns belong to you, Jesus! Anything I've ever done is because you did it through me! Any good I've done is because you're good! Any soul I've ever won is all because of you! It's all you, all the time! It's all because of you! You alone are worthy! Jesus, you alone are my reward!

I live for that day.

PROPHETIC WORD

As we end our time together, I want to speak this prophetic word over your life:

> *A holy invasion is coming upon the daughters of the Lord. Just as there have been historic revivals that affected specific people groups* (a region or nation, college students, Muslims, weary pastors, etc.), *you are part of a coming revival of women who will answer God's call on their lives as you accept His call to advance the Kingdom.*
>
> *A great multitude of women will arise from the sidelines, apathy, the injured players list, fear, lack of support, and the shame of their past to win the lost, disciple the saved, heal the sick, and cast out demons. With golden sickles in hand, they will preach the gospel, stand in five-fold ministry offices, walk in their areas of ministry specialization, and do great exploits for the Lord.*
>
> *They will labor in God's ripe harvest field and stand on the formerly unoccupied placeholders reserved for them since the foundation of the world. They will take back what the enemy has stolen, stand in the gap in intercession, hold up the banner of holiness, push back the darkness, and contend for revival.*
>
> *This company of women leaders will speak with authority, project the blessing on the next generation, tear down strongholds, and declare freedom for the captives. No cost will be too great for these daughters of the living God, for they will eagerly accept the necessary sacrifices in order to blaze trails for the Lord Jesus Christ and fearlessly march forward through every attack of the enemy.*
>
> *These women of God are the true definition of overcomers, and great will be their influence on the earth!*

Woman of God, it's time to gather a vast harvest of souls!
It's time to answer the fullness of God's call!
Now go forth in God's mighty power!
TRAILBLAZER, ARISE!

ABOUT THE AUTHOR

Dr. Jamie Morgan is an ordained minister who has been in ministry for decades as a senior pastor, teacher of the Word, evangelist, revivalist, reformer, a prophetic voice, conference speaker, podcaster, TV show host, and mentor.

She is the author of four previous books—her most recent being *Thirsty: A 31-Day Journey to Personal Revival*—and writes for Charisma and other publications around the world. Her podcast, *Fire Starter* on the Charisma Podcast Network is rated in the top one percent of podcasts globally. She is a member of America's National Prayer Committee.

Dr. Jamie is the founder of *Trailblazer Mentoring Network* (TrailblazerMentoring.com), a mentoring movement for women in ministry. From her many years of ministry experience, she inspires, encourages, and challenges women in ministry to walk in the fullness of their callings.

Her life's mission is to evangelize the nations, call the Church back to the place of prayer, fan the flame of revival, and mentor women called to ministry to set the world ablaze for Jesus Christ. Jamie Morgan's life verse is, *"He* [Paul] *proclaimed the kingdom of God and taught about the Lord Jesus Christ—with all boldness and without hindrance!"* (Acts 28:31 NIV). This is the ministry legacy she desires to leave.

She obtained her Master's degree in Practical Theology from Oral Roberts University and Doctor of Ministry from the Assemblies of God Theological Seminary.

Dr. Jamie Morgan is a wife, mother, and grandmother.

Her website is JamieMorgan.com.